The
EXISTENTIAL
DILEMMA

The
EXISTENTIAL
DILEMMA

Overcoming Intrinsic Anxiety

Donald W. Ogard

To order additional books:
www.amazon.com

For questions, information, or to order bulk copies, contact:
theexistentialdilemma@gmail.com

ISBN: 978-1-952943-20-1

E-book also available

Editorial and Book Packaging: Inspira Literary Solutions, Gig Harbor, WA
Front Cover Design: Lauren Winkle

Printed in the USA

For my grandchildren

Lauren Marie Ogard Winkle
Madeleine Kathleen Ogard
Ethan AhKing Ogard
Hayden Alexandra Skoch
Matthew James Ogard
Olivia Anne Ogard
Karsten Robert Skoch
Grant Wallace Ogard
Carson Robert Aurelius Ogard
Abigail Grace Ogard

Table of Contents

Acknowledgments

The book you hold in your hands is the result of a promise made and a promise kept. I am not normally an emotive person, but I would like to express my deep gratitude to the people who contributed in big and small ways to bring this book to fruition. You all have helped me fulfill Don's wish that this book would be published. Don would be thrilled with the result!

I'd like to extend a special thanks to Inspira Literary Solutions. Arlyn Lawrence was endlessly patient and helpful throughout the process of making change after change in the manuscript. Her expertise, insights, and guidance were so helpful; we couldn't have done this without her and her team. Chelsea Greenwood at Inspira was a thorough proofreader. Many sincere thanks to both of them.

Don was grateful for the many long philosophical and religious conversations he had with my brother, Lowell Hinrichs, and with our four children, Jon, Joel, Kristin, and Erik. Those conversations over a period of years helped him clarify his thinking and strengthen his resolve to leave his philosophical and faith legacy for his grandchildren.

Thank you, Erik, for writing the Faith chapter from Don's extensive handwritten notes, and thank you Joel, Kristin, and Erik for patiently reading the manuscript and making suggestions for improvement.

A special note of thanks to Grant Ogard, who holds a degree in Physics and critiqued the scientific information in the book. Your input was valuable and important.

Very personal illustrations were created by Jon Ogard, Joel Ogard, Lowell Hinrichs, and Lauren Winkle. Thanks to all of you, and thank you, Lauren, for your personal expertise as an independent graphic designer. The cover you designed is beautiful!

Finally, I would like to thank Don, my husband of 65 years, for his strong faith and commitment, for his creative and inquisitive mind, and for his desire to tackle the Existential Dilemma and leave a legacy of hope for those who carry the weight of intrinsic anxiety. Your book and legacy are a beautiful testament to your life and faith, and I am grateful for our life together.

Kathleen Ogard
December 5, 2022

Foreword

My husband Don watched the worldview of society change over the course of his 91 years from a view that accepted faith and religion into a world dominated by a materialistic viewpoint based on science. He wanted to leave his grandchildren a statement about his personal faith as his legacy to them. Don hoped his book would not only help readers understand the Existential Dilemma but, far more importantly, help them acquire or strengthen faith in Jesus as their personal Savior. Don's message to his grandchildren and other readers—now a book, which you are holding in your hands—began as an essay and grew over the years as he continued to learn and express his beliefs and knowledge.

Don was attracted to quantum physics because it provides a new paradigm that gives plausibility to religious beliefs. This is true especially for those people who, based largely on a Newtonian view of the world, have concluded that religious beliefs are implausible. Quantum physics expands the things we know beyond the Newtonian view of our universe. Don saw and understood that the majority of people in our society still view the world of reality as that which can be seen, touched, experienced, or shown by a microscope or telescope.

He was intensely interested in exploring all that he could about the Existential Dilemma. He believed that materialists view anxiety as situational when actually it is basic, common to all people in all time—an inborn anxiety inextricable from the fact of being human beings. It is an innate condition, unavoidable! Even Christ experienced anxiety, as do all humans, but he overcame the Existential Dilemma through his birth, life, and especially his resurrection.

Don felt strongly about all of this and spent many hours reading, studying, and writing, especially after his retirement. He tried to condense his considerable knowledge into a short, easy-to-understand thesis. A number of people have expressed their desire to have a copy of the book. Most of them are Christians, but Don would be pleased if others would also be willing to read it.

Kathleen Ogard
November 1, 2022

How to Read
This Book

Don was passionate about this subject matter, and it was his greatest desire that he would leave behind a learning tool for his children, grandchildren, and anyone else interested in learning more about the intrinsic nature of the Existential Dilemma and its resultant unavoidable anxiety. The breadth of information covered in the book spans many disciplines and should be of interest to a wide variety of readers.

As you read this book, you will notice that Don heavily used asterisks and footnotes in his writing. The asterisks (*) mark words that that he wanted the reader to look up in the glossary at the end of the book to understand their meaning in the context in which he used them. The footnotes (1,2,3, etc.) mark the names of important figures in history, whether they were philosophers, psychologists,* theologians or others who contributed to the research, writing, and dissemination of many of the ideas found in this book.

We encourage you not to skip the glossary or the footnotes. If you don't want to slow down the first time through, we hope you will read it a second time, more slowly, absorbing the ideas and referencing the footnotes and glossary. This would best fulfill the way Don hoped his book would be read and absorbed.

Then, talk about the ideas. Explore them with other people who are interested in them. If you are a person of prayer, pray about them. Invite God into your questioning and exploration. After all the Bible promises us, "If any of you lacks wisdom, let him ask of God, who gives generously and without reproach, and it will be given to him" (James 1:5), and, "Ask, and it will be given to you: seek, and you will find; knock, and it will be opened to you. For everyone who asks receives, and the one who seeks finds and to the one who knocks it will be opened" (Matthew 7:7-8). If you are not a person of faith, we believe you will find the book to be interesting and insightful; it is well worth the read!

Don would be very happy to know that his writings have been published and that he might play a small part in helping others to understand the Existential Dilemma and find answers to it in their own lives. We hope you will enjoy his journey as much as he did.

The Ogard Family
December 16, 2022

The Great Divide

CHAPTER ONE

The Great Divide

"Modern thought has its own dualism.
It treats only the physical world as
knowable and testable, while locking out
everything else—mind, spirit, morality,
meaning—the so-called fact-value split."
~NANCY PEARCEY

N ever in the annals of human history has mankind known
so much but understood so little. There was a time after
Isaac Newton[1] during which the scientific community believed it
understood the workings of the world. The earth was believed to
be measurable and predictable, much like the workings of a clock.
Since the early 1900s and up to the present time, this certainty
of "knowing" has largely evaporated, and "understanding" has
become even more elusive. For example, human consciousness* is

---

1. Newton, Sir Isaac, 1642–1727. English astronomer, physicist, author,
theologian; key figure in the philosophical movement known as the
Enlightenment.

recognized as foundational* to all knowing and yet science doesn't have a clue regarding its origins or even what consciousness is.

Evolutionists* describe the origin of life as a random occurrence but have demonstrated no real understanding of how life began. Quantum physics* informs us that 95 percent of the universe is composed of "dark matter"* and "dark energy,"* but scientists don't actually understand what dark matter and dark energy are. The point I am trying to make is that there is an ever-widening gap between what is *known* and what is *understood*.

Life presents many mysteries. Among them is one that is a central theme of this book, which I refer to as the "Existential Dilemma."* The impact of the dilemma on life and living challenges the human mind to create defensive measures and to seek a solution to what is viewed as a catastrophic situation. No one has managed to discover a solution to this dilemma, since the realities of life are encapsulated* in chronic threats to life and living. The end result is death. Other than creation being marvelous and beautiful, many people fail to find any purpose or meaning to a life that ends in futility.

In spite of the apparent influences of this dilemma, I propose a transcendent* message of hope. It is a centuries-old message that reveals its timelessness and cogency* when its light is shined on the Existential Dilemma. This is the good news, the gospel in the person of Jesus Christ. This message is embedded* in what Jesus did and what he said about himself and his mission.

I believe this is how the Existential Dilemma can be overcome. To the accepting person is gifted a triumphant faith that affirms* the transcendent consciousness and nullifies the power of anxiety* and death. This is a radical* statement because the ideas and concepts presented here are radical in terms of what is currently understood about the dilemma. If the ideas presented here are true, they are valid across time and space.

It must be kept in mind that the Existential Dilemma is a radical problem of the first order. Ultraradical problems require ultraradical answers.

Where We Are Today

Over the course of the past several centuries, Western culture rose to become the dominant influence in the societies of all the developed nations in the world. A sweeping view of history over the last 10,000 years reveals the progressive changes that have evolved to create this situation, which many believe to be in jeopardy in these current days.

To better understand where we find ourselves today, let's take a brief look at some of the major factors that led us here.

The ancient cultures of Sumer, Babylonia, and Egypt developed systems that made collective life possible. These systems necessarily included agricultural development, language creation, governing forms, and laws for protection against enemies and the elements. Mythical* and religious ideas were created to cope with the mysterious or the unknown.

The ancient cultures of Greece and Rome developed and refined these foundational systems; their influence spread throughout the lands surrounding the Mediterranean Sea. Then, approximately two thousand years ago, Jesus of Nazareth appeared on the scene in a small country bordering the Mediterranean. His teachings profoundly* influenced Western culture in all of its aspects, including a new understanding of life's meaning and purpose. Since that time, the population of the world has grown exponentially,* and this growth has led to the formation of many new nations.

The discovery by Europeans of the continents of North and South America between 1500 AD* and 1800 AD spread European ideas and also created manifold* developments that have revolutionized the way people live and think. Prior to this, transformative influences began to occur in the European nations in the 13th and 14th centuries, leading to the Renaissance* and then the Enlightenment.* The dynamics of this period permeated all aspects of Western civilization, giving impetus to the creative powers of the human intellect. The liberation* message of the Christian faith planted the concept of human freedom into art, architecture,* music, and education. The Gutenberg printing press, developed in 1454, enabled the general public to participate in the flowering and expansion of knowledge. What, then, was the main reason for the subsequent dominance of Western culture in the entire civilized world?

To answer this question, we must identify the most significant philosophy* in its development. Simply stated, that philosophy is humanistic materialism,* which emerged from the growing preeminence of science and the scientific method of determining "truth." The importance of science cannot be overstated in understanding how Western culture came to dominance in the world.

How the West Won

The revolution that began in the 15th century produced men of early science like Copernicus,[2] Galileo Galilei,[3] and Kepler,[4] who laid the foundations for subsequent scientific discovery. It was the creative genius of such unique individuals that determined the pivotal* points of cultural evolution. Among this group of creative thinkers were two men who revolutionized the pathway leading to Western dominance. One was philosopher/mathematician René Descartes;[5] the other was physicist/mathematician Sir Isaac Newton.[6] The difference in the ages of these men precluded any personal contact between them, but the combined influence of their thinking created what has come to be called "The Great Divide,"* or the "Mind-Body Split."

Perhaps the most significant influence was the philosophical rendering of Descartes. He is primarily responsible for the division between what is subjective* and what is objective.* This philosophical divide continued its influence in the philosophical

---

2. Copernicus, Nicolaus, 1473–1543, astronomer, instrumental in establishing the system in which the sun rather than the earth is the center of our solar system.

3. Galilei, Galileo, 1564–1642, astronomer, physicist, and engineer, called the "Father of modern physics," or "Father of the scientific method."

4. Kepler, Johannes, 1571–1630, astronomer, natural philosopher, and musician best known for his laws of planetary motion.

5. Descartes, René, 1596–1650, creative mathematician, scientific thinker, metaphysician, generally regarded as the founder of modern philosophy.

6. Newton, Sir Isaac, 1642–1727, English astronomer, physicist, author, theologian, key figure in the philosophical movement known as The Enlightenment.

systems of the idealistic* versus the materialistic.* Some refer to this as "the bifurcation."* This philosophical divide has given rise to the perennial debate over the mind-body relationship. Descartes referred to it as *res cogitantes** (thinking entities) and *res extensae** (extended entities). It was his determined search for certainty that led to his philosophical conclusions.

Mathematics provided certainty for the arena of *res extensae* (extended entities), and he sought to duplicate this in the arena of *res cogitantes* (thinking entities). His method was to doubt everything. His conclusion was that everything could be doubted except his thinking (doubting is still thinking). Descartes' statement *"Cogito ergo sum"* is world-famous, and the world initially accepted it: "I think, therefore I am."

What has been the fallout of this Cartesianism?* What Descartes established as the certainty of mental processes developed into an irony of the profound. His ideas were thrust into an intellectual community seemingly bound by the union of the mind-body complex but also primed and open to scientific revelation.* The religious fathers held firmly to the unity of the mind-body complex, while the materialists freely accepted the divide.

This viewpoint prevailed and allowed the church, because of *res cogitantes* (thinking entities), to be the locus* of thinking about theology and freed science (*res extensae*) to be the arbiter* of the physical domain.* It was as if the thinking self became enclosed in its own ivory tower, leaving the material world ever free and open to exploration without residue.* In other words, it meant the church no longer played a significant role in scientific matters and left the workings of the material world open to scientific discoveries.

During the same era, the world was introduced to one of the greatest minds in the history of science. Sir Isaac Newton, a key figure in the philosophical movement known as the Enlightenment, astounded the world with his discoveries and his perception* of the physical cosmos.* With his genius, the material world became the realm of certainty, predictability, and fundamental reality. The earth and the cosmos became a clockwork universe.

For nearly 400 years, materialism has remained the prevailing scientific force, revolutionizing life on Earth. The harnessing of the forces* of electricity and petroleum has created manifold changes in the everyday lives of all people everywhere. We now travel the earth on the ground and in the air in vehicles undreamed of a mere 150 years ago. We communicate person-to-person with information traveling at the speed of light. The listing of revolutionary inventions could go on and on nearly *ad infinitum.** Truly, the achievements of science have been spectacular, and currently, the sphere of materialism dominates the human psyche.*

During this era of the dominance of materialism, Descartes' *res cogitantes* have been relegated to the background of influence in intellectual and artistic pursuits. Its influence continues to diminish even further and gives obeisance* to the dominant *res extensa.* This effect is noticeable in art (cubism), music (discordance), design (asymmetry), and literature (existential* futility).

The growing rejection of religion in Europe, and in other areas of our world, has coincided with the increasing acceptance of materialism as the dominant force guiding the understanding of reality. Consequently, the Christian message of salvation is viewed as dubious and is therefore dismissed: "Pie in the sky, by and by," as my generation used to say. Religion appears to be irrelevant compared to the relevance and immediacy of Newton's clockwork reality; the Christian message of human brokenness and the need to be "saved" have been increasingly relegated to the areas of superstition and ignorance. According to currently prevalent thinking, if any saving of humanity is necessary, science and the scientific method will discover the truth, and reality will be changed for the better in a predictable manner. The humanists believe their quest for the perfectibility of humans and a utopian* world will become a real probability.* But . . . I ask, "Is this just more "Pie in the sky, by and by"?

The consequence of Cartesianism, the Great Divide, has seemingly introduced a permanent split in the historic unity of subject and object in our human perceptions of reality. Something doesn't seem to jibe here. Human persons are obviously a unified composite of subject and object. The English language verifies* this in its design for navigating the realities of living by the use of subject, verb, and object. For example, consider this sentence: "I think about my body." "I" is the subject, "think" is the verb, and "my body" is the object. The subject and the object are a unified duality,* helping to create a complete thought. If the human being is the locus of unified duality, then the permanence of the divide can be questioned and challenged.

Materialism has not resolved the mysteries of life. In fact, the progressive discoveries of science in the late 19th century and 20th centuries radically upended the foundations of Newtonian physics.* The certainty and predictability of the foundations of materialism have evaporated like dew before the rising sun.

Recently, the mystery of the nature of consciousness has appeared on the scene as a ghost from the past. Long ignored by science, it has made its debut in the revelations of quantum physics. A discussion of these revelations will follow in the chapters ahead as we dive into the concept of the Existential Dilemma.

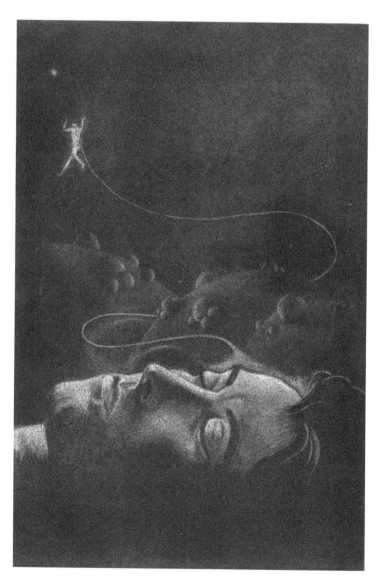

Consciousness

CHAPTER TWO

Consciousness

*"Consciousness is the most mysterious
phenomenon in the universe."*
~DAVID CHALMERS

*"The hard problem of consciousness
cannot be solved."*
~BERNARDO KASTRUP

The study of consciousness has been released from its dormancy!* Ignored for centuries, scientists have now discovered that consciousness is intimately connected to the microcosm* and therefore plays a definite role in all physical realities. This phenomenon* has surfaced through the discoveries of quantum physics, and science must now devote serious effort to unfolding its mysteries.

Currently, the study of consciousness is developing across the globe with literally thousands of physicists, neurobiologists,* and philosophers joining the parade of researchers. Will the mystery of consciousness now be explained? Will the great divide between thinking entities and extended entities (the physical cosmos) be reunited? The understanding of consciousness will become a key factor in the answers to these questions.

Consciousness plays a central role in the formation of this thesis.* It is foundational to the concept of the Existential Dilemma that is inherent* in all of human experience. (This premise* will be unfolded in the chapters that follow.) Our intuition,* the immediate awareness of the obvious, informs us of the certainty that consciousness is real and seems to be located somewhere in the brain. How this happens is a mystery. Theories abound but understanding remains totally elusive.

Journalist George Will[1] expressed the mystery of consciousness succinctly* in a newspaper editorial on August 26, 2013. In it, he asked the following question: "How does matter become conscious of itself?" "Or," he added, "how does it become conscious?" These are the unanswered questions.

The speculation of theorists runs the gamut of denial that consciousness is a reality to the concept of the brain producing consciousness through quantum dynamics.* This much appears to be realistic, namely that the brain is actively involved in consciousness. Is there more? Yes! Emphatically, *yes*! To gain a foothold of understanding, I propose that there are three qualities of consciousness to be considered:

---

1. Will, George, b. 1941, American libertarian-conservative political commentator and author, Pulitzer Prize winner for commentary in 1977.

- ▶ Consciousness is subjective.
- ▶ Consciousness is transcendent.
- ▶ Consciousness presents itself as being dualistic* (that is, the condition of being double—the self is conscious of being conscious).

Consciousness Is Subjective

The first consideration of importance is that consciousness has never been defined satisfactorily. There is a very good explanation for this: consciousness is completely and totally subjective. This means that it cannot be construed as an object. Objects occupy the time/space realm, are physical, can be measured, and therefore can be defined. Consciousness meets none of these qualifications. The experience of consciousness is subjective, ethereal,* or spiritual, without physical presence.

Consciousness Is Transcendent

*"He has made everything beautiful in its time;
also He has put eternity into man's mind,
yet so that he cannot find out what God
has done from the beginning to the end."*
~ECCLESIASTES 3:11

The second important quality for consideration is that consciousness is transcendent over time and space. This means that it preserves superiority over everything it observes. My old college professor, Dr. JP Pflueger, put it succinctly: "I can think about Pluto, but Pluto can't think about me!"

To describe the transcendent quality of consciousness presents a challenge to our use of language. We use words in an attempt to provide clear understanding of objects and events occurring in the world of existence. Analogies* compare things that are alike in some ways but are different. We often use them to provide an explanation of a concept. To portray the notion of transcendence, I will therefore use analogies.

Suppose, for example, that you are located in an enclosed, windowless room. Suddenly the electric power fails, the lights turn off, and you are thrust into total darkness. Nothing is visible. Everything is impenetrable darkness. Then you remember that you have a flashlight in the satchel you are carrying. You turn on the flashlight, and presto! The flashlight illuminates the room, and you can orient yourself to the space and the objects within it. The light has overcome the darkness and therefore is transcendent over it.

In this analogy, the light produced by the flashlight symbolizes consciousness. As this light illuminates the room and its objects, so consciousness illuminates the time/space reality. Without consciousness there is only the darkness of nothingness.* With consciousness, the perception of physical reality is revealed. As light overcomes darkness, consciousness overcomes what it observes.

Analogies like these are not guarantees of proof, but they do appeal to our intuition. Consciousness, being totally subjective, cannot be considered a candidate for scientific proof.

Intuition informs us that events of every moment of life move through the continuum* of time and space. However, without consciousness, events happen and instantaneously become history. They seem to come from the future and become the past with no possible observation of the transition. Where is the sense of the present?

Logic proclaims that the present, therefore, does not exist. Personal experience, however, definitely confirms that the present, the here and now, is everywhere around us and follows us wherever we go. We exist in a reality of the present as the arrow of time moves through space. We observe beginnings and endings within this realm, witness movement and change, and perceive it as the "present." It's as if consciousness interjects itself between the past and the future and creates our sense of the present.

Is it transcendent consciousness that creates the perception of the present? What else could it be?

Consciousness Is Dualistic

A third quality of consciousness to consider is self-awareness. Not only is consciousness "conscious"; it is *aware* of being conscious. This suggests a nature of duality. A mind can think something and critically examine its own thinking. This quality of consciousness enables a person to have a relationship with the "self" and establishes the sentience* of freedom and analytic ability.

A perceptual challenge arises with the concept of duality because duality is experienced as a singularity.* How can this be? Language languishes in attempting to describe this phenomenon, so I will use illustrations and analogies to help portray these difficult concepts.

I have presented three considerations of consciousness, with qualities of being subjective, transcendent, and dualistic. Together these qualities create a functional concept of consciousness. The first two suggest an independent status* of being, their single identity. The third suggests the nature of relationship between the two identities of self and self-awareness and a dynamic reciprocity* between the two identities.

Since we experience consciousness as an active process, my focus will be on the strong influence of the dualistic nature of consciousness, which portrays its ability to interconnect with all aspects of consciousness. Consciousness fuses all aspects of subjectivity and transcendence, resulting in a singular* experience. For example, you are aware of yourself reading about this topic.

Before proceeding further with a theoretical* description of how consciousness functions, it may be helpful to gain some insights from one of the foremost experts in the study of consciousness. David Chalmers[2] is the author of two widely acclaimed books, *The Conscious Mind* (1996) and *The Character of Consciousness* (2010). The following excerpts are from a TED Talk by Chalmers, recorded around 2016. Chalmers openly acknowledges the mystery of consciousness and seeks a scientific solution to the problem. This, he speculates, may be found in the transmission of information.

---

2. Chalmers, David, PhD, b. 1966, Australian philosopher and cognitive scientist. Professor of philosophy and neuroscience at New York University.

"Some people say a science of consciousness is impossible. Science, by its nature, is objective. Consciousness, by its nature, is subjective. So, there can never be a science of consciousness. For much of the 20th century, that view held sway. Psychologists studied behavior objectively; neuroscientists studied the brain objectively, and nobody even mentioned consciousness. Even 30 years ago, when TED got started, there was very little scientific work on consciousness.

"Now, I'm a scientific materialist at heart. I want a scientific theory of consciousness that works, and for a long time I banged my head against the wall looking for a theory of consciousness, in purely physical terms, that would work. But I eventually came to the conclusion that that just didn't work for systematic reasons.

"It's a long story, but the core idea is just that what you get from purely reductionist* explanations in physical behavior—in physical terms, in brain-based terms—is stories about the functioning of a system, its structures,* its dynamics, and the behavior it produces, which is great for solving the easy problems (how we behave, how we function), but when it comes to subjective experience, why does all this feel like something from the inside? That's something fundamentally new, and it's always a further question.

"So I think that we're at a kind of impasse here. We've got this wonderful, great explanation—we're used to it—where physics explains chemistry, chemistry explains biology, biology explains parts of psychology.* But consciousness doesn't seem to fit into this picture. On the one hand, it's a datum*

that we're conscious. On the other hand, we don't know how to accommodate it into our scientific view of the world. So, I think consciousness right now is a kind of anomaly, one that needs to integrate into our view of the world, but we don't yet see how. Faced with an anomaly like this, radical ideas may be needed, and I think that we may need one or two ideas that initially seem crazy before we can come to grips with consciousness scientifically.*

"The first crazy idea is that consciousness is fundamental. Physicists sometimes take some aspects of the universe as fundamental building blocks: space and time and mass.* They postulate fundamental laws governing them, like the laws of gravity or of quantum mechanics.* These fundamental properties and laws aren't explained in terms of anything more basic. Rather, they are taken as primitive, and you build up the world from there.

"Now, sometimes, the list of fundamentals expands. In the 19th century, Maxwell figured out that you can't explain electromagnetic phenomena in terms of the existing fundamentals—space, time, mass, Newton's laws—so he postulated fundamental laws of electromagnetism and postulated electric charge as a fundamental element that those laws govern. I think that's the situation we're in with consciousness. If you can't explain consciousness in terms of the existing fundamentals—space, time, mass, charge—then as a matter of logic, you need to expand the list.

"The natural thing to do is to postulate consciousness itself as something fundamental, a fundamental building* block of nature. This doesn't mean you suddenly can't do science with it. This opens up the way for you to do science with it. What we then need to do is to study the fundamental laws governing consciousness, the laws that connect consciousness to other fundamentals: space, time, mass, physical processes. Physicists sometimes say that we want fundamental laws so simple we could write them on the front of a t-shirt. We don't know what those laws are yet, but that's what we're after.

"The second crazy idea is that consciousness might be universal. Every system might have some degree of consciousness. This view is sometimes called panpsychism*—'pan' for all, 'psych' for mind—every system is conscious, not just humans, dogs, mice, flies, but even Rob Knight's microbes, elementary particles.* Even a photon* has some degree of consciousness. The idea is not that photons are intelligent or thinking. It is not that a photon is wracked with angst because it is thinking, 'Aw, I'm always buzzing around near the speed of light. I never get to slow down and smell the roses.' No, not like that. But the thought is maybe photons might have some element of raw, subjective feeling, some primitive precursor to consciousness.

"A deeper motivation comes from the idea that perhaps the most simple and powerful way to find fundamental laws connecting consciousness to physical processing is to link consciousness to information. Wherever there's information processing, there's consciousness. Complex information processing is, like in a human, complex consciousness. Simple information processing, simple consciousness."

The mystery of consciousness rests in obscurity. Researchers continue to probe the brain for clues that might shed light on how a lumpy glob of gray matter can produce consciousness. Previously I identified three qualities that characterize consciousness: subjectivity, transcendence, and duality. None of these qualities project even slight evidence of a material base or origin. And yet the brain certainly presents itself as an organ of consciousness.

The dualistic aspect of self-awareness suggests the presence of a second quality. David Chalmers seems to hint at such a possibility in his labeling consciousness as fundamental and universal. Does he mean fundamental as physically present and universal as cosmologically present? He doesn't say. This would seem to introduce metaphysics* and philosophy into the mystery. It certainly opens the door to speculation.

Chalmers' two qualities could be understood to introduce the concepts of finitude* and infinitude.* The physical brain equates with the finite* while the transcendent consciousness equates with the infinite. It is my viewpoint that consciousness incorporates* both qualities of the finite and the infinite into a unified duality. This is not a foreign idea in nature. Consider, for instance, how hydrogen and oxygen combine to form water.

Where Does Consciousness Originate?

Let's look at a few more analogies and illustrations to help us wrap our minds around these ideas. I am proposing that consciousness originates from a source external to the human brain. In current scientific literature I am not aware of such an idea, but it certainly qualifies as a "crazy" radical idea, as referenced by David Chalmers.

The organic brain is a marvel of complexity. There are estimated to be 100 billion cells (neurons*) that compose a functioning brain. I believe it is reasonable to describe the brain as a receiver, processor, and sender of information. Consciousness certainly accompanies these brain functions, but "from whence cometh consciousness?" To postulate that consciousness originates from a source exterior to the brain may be a radical idea to many. However, I believe the concept is not foreign to either nature or human experience.

Cell phones, radios, televisions, and computers are all devices that depend on exterior sources of information. These instruments are receivers, decoders, and senders of information that originates from transmitters* far away. It's the electromagnetic force,* namely radio waves, that carries the coded data to the receiving instrument.

Similarly, consider vision: photons bounce off objects and enter the lens of the eye, dependent on light; they are the particles that carry light, focusing on the retina of the eyeball, which is directly connected to the brain's visual center. Without universal microscopic photons, no vision would be possible.

These particles of light occupy a very narrow range of the electromagnetic spectrum and are present everywhere in the cosmos, traveling at 186,242 miles per second. The visual process clearly demonstrates the brain's dependency on a source of information exterior to itself. The eye does not create light. It receives it and transmits* it to the brain, where it is interpreted as light.

Photosynthesis* presents another illustration of exterior dependency. Photons of light shine down on the earth and bathe green vegetation with life-giving nurture. The leaves of trees and plants are sensitive to the photon energy and use it to power the breakdown of carbon dioxide and water into oxygen, sugar, and starch. Without photons, vegetation cannot exist. Without vegetation, life cannot exist. Life is dependent upon an external source—light!

On July 4, 2012, physicists announced from Geneva, Switzerland that the so-called "God particle"* had been discovered. This particle is officially known as the Higgs boson* and was theoretically proposed in the 1960s by physicist Peter Higgs,[3] among others. This discovery is heralded as one of the greatest events in quantum physics history. Why? Because it reveals how mass and matter are created!

Many particles are involved in what is called a decaying and transforming process. This process is exceedingly complex and the details are not important for this illustration. It is, however, important to note that the creation of the Higgs boson occurs in the atmosphere 10 to 20 miles above ground level. It is the product of the Higgs field* located throughout the entire cosmos. All matter originates by this process, and all of life is vitally dependent on the boson. The discoveries of quantum physics are revealing how dependent life is on sources exterior to its being.

There is one further illustration to be considered in this theory that consciousness is created outside the brain. To this point, I

---

3. Higgs, Peter, b. 1929, British theoretical physicist, Nobel Laureate for his work on the mass of subatomic particles.

have used some analogies to demonstrate how radios, televisions, and computers are activated by radio waves, how vision is activated by photons, how vegetation is dependent on photosynthesis, and how the mass created by the Higgs boson is dependent on a cosmological field. To be able to function, each of these systems relies on energy sources external to their structure. Likewise, I am proposing that the brain and its consciousness are dependent on an exterior source of energy, possibly the neutrino.*

What Is a Neutrino?

Quantum physics has established that four forces of nature comprise the material universe. They are the electromagnetic force, gravity,* the strong force,* and the weak force.* Neutrinos are products of the weak force and are governed by it. They come into existence through a complicated process of the spontaneous decay of neutrons,* pions,* and muons* in space. Neutrinos are tiny, pinpoint particles but are unique in their form, are of miniscule mass (if any), and have no electrical charge. They are stable and considered to be indestructible. In other words, they are considered to be infinite.

Neutrinos move throughout the cosmos at the speed of light, penetrating with ease everything they encounter, including Planet Earth. According to physicist Paul Davies,[4] light-years of lead would be no challenge to them; they would pass through it with

4. Davies, Paul, b. 1946, English physicist, professor at Arizona State University, affiliated with the Institute for Quantum Studies at Chapman University in California.

ease. Neutrinos are created by supernova* explosions and by the process of fusion* in stars. This includes our own sun, which is the earth's major source of neutrinos. Physicists estimate that two hundred billion neutrinos pass through the human body every second. Enrico Fermi[5] named the neutrino, which in Italian means "the little one."

There are some interesting reasons why the neutrino appeals to me as a possible activating source of consciousness. I have described the nature of consciousness as transcendent and as a unified duality. This "nature" suggests an integration* or fusion* process between two sources of energy that bond to create the experience of consciousness within a person. The electrochemical energy of the brain is well understood and documented. What is not understood is how the brain achieves its transcendent nature.

The structure of the brain is composed of matter. To create the capacity of transcendence, the conscious brain must produce an energy source not limited to time and space and yet present within its boundaries. Consider the qualities of the neutrino. It is ubiquitous—everywhere in space. It is a particle without structure, described as an infinitesimal point. Yet, it has to have a miniscule amount of mass to have a material presence. Perhaps it could potentially activate transcendent consciousness. Its essential nature is transcendence; nothing contains a neutrino.

The physical brain is encased in a bony structure, the skull. Obviously, the neutrino has no difficulty penetrating the skull,

---

5. Fermi, Enrico, 1901–1942, Italian-born naturalized American citizen, physicist, creator of the world's first nuclear reactor.

and this includes the tissue of the brain. Also, it appears to have enough mass to be experienced by the brain cells. Could this neutrino be the activating force that provides the brain its transcendent nature?

It penetrates* and is nondestructive. It has zero electric charge, which could mean it would have no capacity to disrupt the electrochemical dynamics of the brain function. If the brain cells were structured with sensors that vibrated or resonated to the neutrinos' penetrating presence, could this create the unified duality of consciousness?

Roger Penrose[6] and Stuart Hameroff[7] have proposed that tubules* found in brain cells serve a purpose in creating consciousness. Admittedly this is speculation but, on the other hand, isn't this where the understanding of reality begins? My intuition tells me that the neutrino is a candidate to be studied as a possible creator and activator of an individual's consciousness and could be a potential field of study for physicists. Could the microtubules* in brain cells be receptors of the passage of neutrinos?

I intend for these intuitive and theoretical concepts to demonstrate the transcendent nature of consciousness and its preeminence in life, and to support its universal and foundational position. I hope you can grasp the possibility that our brains are

---

6. Penrose, Roger, b. 1931, British mathematical physicist, philosopher of science, Nobel Laureate in physics.
7. Hameroff, Stuart, b. 1947, American anesthesiologist, professor at University of Arizona, known for studies of consciousness, originator of the contention that consciousness originates from quantum states in neural microtubules.

not the creators of our consciousness, but rather that we are reliant on an external cosmological source. This premise is important because it sets the stage for identifying and dealing with the human Existential Dilemma.

As we will discover and discuss in the chapters ahead, consciousness is the host of a most unwelcome partner that many of us know all too well, namely *anxiety.*

Quiescence

CHAPTER THREE

The Existential Dilemma

"If a kingdom is divided against itself,
that kingdom cannot stand."
~MARK 3:24

On Sunday morning, May 18th, 1980, Mount Saint Helens in Southwest Washington State, about 40 miles north of Portland, Oregon, USA, exploded with a vengeance—a spectacle that seldom occurs in North America. Before the eruption, Mount Saint Helens was a beautiful, snow-clad jewel, rising majestically above the Cascade Mountain range.

Metaphorically,* a volcano such as Mount Saint Helens can symbolize human beings and their anxiety: beautiful on the outside but harboring potential destructive power on the inside. Although a volcano may appear to be at rest, its very essence* is explosive as its magma grows under the surface. Within its core, the possibility of eruption remains.

So it is with the human psyche, where anxiety rests at times in tranquility and yet at other times can burst forth in an overwhelming eruption of despair and violence. Even in its quietude,* anxiety can emerge within a person's consciousness as a warning of possible danger, thus creating a mild experience of anxiety. However, in chronic or extreme conditions, the presence of anxiety in one's consciousness can distort the perception of reality and lead to neurosis or sociopathic* behaviors.

The consideration of consciousness continues in this chapter because it occupies a central position in the dynamic formation of the Existential Dilemma. The components of the dilemma form an interrelated triad that creates an enigma* with critical consequences. These components are consciousness, anxiety, and existence. My goal in this chapter is to identify the role that is played by each component and to explain how together they create the Existential Dilemma.

Consciousness

While being the most basic of human experiences, consciousness remains undefined and somewhat "out of this world." *Webster's Dictionary* describes consciousness as "(1) the state of being conscious; awareness of one's own existence, sensations, thoughts, surroundings, etc., (2) the thoughts and feelings, collectively of an individual, or an aggregate of people, and (3) full activity of the mind and senses, as in waking life."

In the previous chapter, I described consciousness as subjective, transcendent, and self-aware. Webster's description appears to support some of this premise, but it lacks any reference to a transcendent nature. In fact, most scientists have refrained from any direct description of consciousness as being transcendent. David Chalmers hints of this possibility when he describes consciousness as universal and foundational; his reference to the "hard problem" of consciousness appears to suggest a transcendent quality. In essence, his description of the "hard problem" is the awareness of what it "feels like" to have a conscious experience. The consciousness of being conscious strongly suggests a duality. Is Chalmers alluding to a transcendent quality?

This begs the question of whether or not transcendent consciousness prevails over its own existential consciousness. The challenge of science is to explain how the physical brain accomplishes this feat. One thing is certain: consciousness is primary in the human experience of life. Without it, there is absolutely nothing to be experienced.

Anxiety

"The basic anxiety, the anxiety of a finite being about the threat of nonbeing, cannot be eliminated. It belongs to existence itself."
~PAUL TILLICH

The way anxiety manifests* itself has not really changed over the centuries. Modern humans are still plagued by the same forms of anxiety disorders as our ancient ancestors—although the things that trigger our anxiety have certainly changed.

We still experience many traditional causes of anxiety, though thankfully, in Western society, many of these factors are on the

The Scream

decline, such as poverty, poor health, and lack of access to basic resources. However, they have been replaced by some entirely new sources of anxiety in our generation and the ones that are coming up under us.

Along with the rash of new, modern anxieties (think social media and its 24/7 connectivity, nonstop communication inputs, emotionally charged news reporting and constant doomsday scenarios, and the COVID-19 pandemic and its related fears and concerns, to name a few), there has been a gradual shift in the social ethos surrounding anxiety. On the one hand, society tells us that anxiety is a legitimate response to the stresses of modern living and is sometimes almost considered a status symbol that signals how busy and successful we are. But, on the other hand, we are led to believe that our anxiety is a misplaced emotion in need of therapy and medication.

During my career as a counselor, I saw the steady increase in clients dealing with anxiety. New diagnostic categories for anxiety problems mounted yearly, and I watched the pharmaceutical industry grow keener and keener to medicate anxiety and reap exponential profits by providing pharmaceutical solutions for it. I witnessed social campaigns (and perhaps you have too) that made an effort to increase public awareness of mental health problems such as anxiety and valiantly attempted to destigmatize it.

But, despite all the best efforts over the history of mankind, anxiety remains a pervasive problem. In his book *The Problem of Anxiety*, Sigmund Freud[1] states: "Anxiety is the fundamental phenomenon and the central problem of Neurosis."* Elsewhere, in his *General Introduction to Psychoanalysis*, he says, "One thing is certain, that the problem of anxiety is the nodal* point, linking up all kinds of important questions, a riddle of which the solution must cast a flood of light upon our whole mental life."

I find agreement with Freud's emphasis on the importance of anxiety and its impact on life. His references to the words "riddle" and "solutions" are also significant. As I have noted, consciousness and anxiety remain a mystery to science.

---

1. Freud, Sigmund, 1856–1939, Austrian neurologist, founder of psychoanalysis.

Webster's Unabridged Encyclopedic Dictionary defines anxiety as "distress or uneasiness of mind caused by fear of danger or misfortune." The included psychiatric definition refers to "a state of apprehension and psychic tension occurring in some forms of mental disorder." These proposed "definitions" portray anxiety as a reaction to situational security threats and therefore place causal dynamics exterior to the person. This implies that anxiety is an aberration from the norm of healthy being. The contention of my thesis is more far-reaching. I view anxiety in all its forms as intrinsic* within consciousness. I do not view basic anxiety as an aberration.

Paul Tillich,[2] the great 20th century theologian/philosopher, in his book, *The Courage to Be*, offers the following ontological* description of anxiety:

> *"Finitude in awareness is anxiety. Like finitude, anxiety is an ontological quality. It cannot be derived; it can only be seen and described. Occasions in which anxiety is aroused must be distinguished from anxiety itself. As an ontological quality, anxiety is as omnipresent* as is finitude. Anxiety is independent of any special object which might produce it; it is dependent only on the* threat *of nonbeing, which is identical with finitude. In this sense, it has been said rightly that the object of anxiety is "nothingness"—and "nothingness" is not an object. Objects can be feared. A danger, a pain, an enemy, may be feared, but fear can be conquered by actions.*

---

2. Tillich, Paul, 1886–1965, Christian existentialist, philosopher, theologian, and author, taught at Union Theological Seminary.

Anxiety cannot, for no finite being can conquer its finitude. Although it is often latent,* anxiety is always present. Therefore it can become manifest in any and every moment, even in situations where nothing is to be feared."

Tillich's statement is very enlightening and worthy of scrutiny. I note that the word "consciousness" is absent. Perhaps it is implied by the word "awareness" in the first sentence. His linkage of anxiety with finitude is correct, but I propose that the linkage with consciousness creates a more profound consequence. Consciousness is transcendent over time and space, while finitude exists in the arena of time and space.

Simply stated, finitude is death: all "things" in this physical world come to an end. The mathematical odds determine this to be a certainty. Death apparently has the power to annihilate consciousness, and this reality is indelibly etched within consciousness. The doorway to the experience of anxiety has been flung open by the power of death, and the invasion is complete. Consciousness is the reluctant host of transcendent anxiety, but it doesn't stop there. Tragically, consciousness becomes and is also the creator of anxiety. The singular experience of consciousness has been forfeited to an overpowering threat, thus forming a paradoxical* nature; consciousness is divided. The opposed sides are both its strength and its weakness.

Each and every human being experiences anxiety. Its nature is profound because it joins consciousness in transcendent power. As noted, consciousness creates the experience of anxiety and also situates itself side by side with consciousness. The power of anxiety demands that consciousness must view existence with a jaundiced eye and a vigilant attitude. This positions a person in a precarious state without absolute control over the past, present, or future.

Human Existence

In the real world, anxiety keeps us mindful of the range of uncertain possibilities that face us every day. It is this uncertainty that plagues consciousness, which is polarized* between the forces of strength and weakness.

Although compromised by anxiety, consciousness can harness its own strength to combat this. With strengths of rationality, reason, willpower, imagination, and creativity, consciousness can learn to cope with inherent weaknesses.

The traits of weakness are ignorance, fear, doubt, self-absorption, and defensive and escapist behaviors. A chronic tension exists between these poles, with the force of anxiety demanding choices that lead to strength. With strength there is less anxiety, but in weakness there is more anxiety. Either way, they each—both strength and weakness—play out their drama within the reality of our existence.

The world in which we exist is a physical realm, filling time and space with myriad objects, large and small, simple and complex. This appears so obvious as to preclude any questions of mystery. We can—and many of us do—live our entire lives giving our attention exclusively to the material domain as the focal point of our reality.

Reality? What is it that enables humans to perceive this reality? It is consciousness—subjective, transcendent consciousness!

This viewpoint opens the concept of reality to the inclusion of the metaphysical world along with the physical world and expands reality to be inclusive of all human experience. (I will address the metaphysical nature of essential consciousness again in Chapter Five and Chapter Eight.)

In this section of the chapter, the focus is on the physical, existing realm. Gazing at the landscape, what do we see? We see a world full of objects: mountains, plains, shrubs, trees, buildings, cars, trucks, airplanes, animals, and people. Each object has dimensions such as height, width, and depth. In addition, all objects exist within the time/space realm that permits their dimensionality.

One object exists, however, that appears to contradict the dichotomous* structure of its form: the perfect sphere. Its dimensions all emanate* from a center point, creating a singular identity. Examining it from any angle reveals an identical appearance with no observable variation in its dimensions. It can always be described as having a constant, unchanging shape viewed from any perspective.*

But a strange development occurs when a perfect sphere spins around an axis:* it becomes polarized. Commonly these axes* are called the north and south poles. By shifting our attention to a spinning earth with its north and south poles, a surprising, even stunning development occurs.

Picture yourself standing on the Arctic Circle looking at the North Pole. From this position, the earth appears to be spinning counterclockwise. Next, picture yourself standing on the Antarctic Circle, looking at the South Pole. From this position, the earth appears to be spinning clockwise. How can this be, since the earth only spins in one direction? Certainly, this presents an enigma and creates the perception that the physical realm is intrinsically divided. A closer examination will demonstrate this to be factually true.

Physicists refer to this "dual" formation of left/right structure resulting from polarization as a mirror image. In all respects, they are identical except that the left/right aspects appear to be reversed and opposite. This unitized opposition is foundational to the entire physical realm and is described by the term "parity,"* which means equivalence or correspondence. Quantum physics also uses the word "symmetry"* to express this concept. All told, this is the everyday experience of living, and most of us take it for granted without so much as a thought. The intrinsic polarity and mirror image formation present no apparent difficulties to our perceptions. It's just the way things are.

As stated, however, it is always consciousness that surveys the physical realm. Consciousness has been identified as being divided between oppositional forces of strength and weakness. We can identify the physical world as existing in a divided state between left/right and mirror imaging. The conclusion must, therefore, be drawn that all reality, both mental and physical, is bifurcated. This means that the human race must chronically face a fork in the road of existence.

What we discover is a reality of ambiguity* and paradoxical understanding that impacts both the subjective and objective nature of living. The dilemma for consciousness is the overpowering threat of death to its supremacy over the physical realm that tragically leads to its demise.* The dilemma for the objective realm is its inheritance of supremacy over the subjective realm, a role it is incapable of fulfilling. The loss of subjective supremacy is a loss of epic magnitude. What materializes leads to human existence encased in transcendent anxiety, meaninglessness, ambiguity, uncertainty, futility, finitude, and ultimate despair. This is the Existential Dilemma!

My, oh my! Such negativity! Somehow, somewhere in this world there must be a solution to the Existential Dilemma. The history of all cultures portrays great efforts to cope with their dilemmas. In the next chapter, we will embark on a brief review of some historical attempts toward resolution.*

The Spiritual Quest

CHAPTER FOUR

The Search for a Solution in Religion

"What a chimera then is man! What a
novelty, what a monster, what a chaos, what
a contradiction, what a prodigy! Judge
of all things, imbecile worm of the earth;
depository of truth, a sink of uncertainty and
error; the pride and refuse of the universe."*
~BLAISE PASCAL

This quote from Blaise Pascal's *Pensées*[1] demonstrates his understanding of the human dilemma with penetrating clarity. It portrays the polarized and paradoxical condition of humanity presented in the previous chapter. I've identified it as

---

1. Pascal, Blaise, 1623–1662, French mathematician, physicist, inventor, philosopher, theologian; laid the foundation for the modern theory of probabilities.

the Existential Dilemma. However, it does not take a genius like Pascal to discover that humans are imperfect specimens.

The Existential Dilemma is the product of the union of anxiety and consciousness. The dilemma acquires its power through the experience of anxiety usurping, undermining, and potentially overwhelming the transcendent consciousness. The human psyche experiences this as inescapable and permanent. It is truly ontological and paradoxical in the sense that conscious awareness becomes both the strength and weakness of humanity.

This dilemma is more far-reaching than the psychic phenomenon alone. It is existential (meaning, it raises questions pertaining to our very existence) and plays its hand in all realms of the physical world. The threats to our lives and limbs are many and often unexpected. Events like natural disasters, accidents, diseases, injuries, etc. can all dramatically change the course of a person's life. What is revealed to us through this understanding of the Existential Dilemma is that its impact on life is overwhelming and is fully psychosocial.*

A Sustained and Catastrophic Impact

Should an alien from another galaxy venture to our planet, it would not take long for him to surmise that humans have problems— serious, serious problems! They murder, lie, cheat, and steal. They are self-centered; they manipulate others and are prone to error. They create conflict and chaos but deny responsibility. Hostility and vengeance are always close at hand.

David Berlinski, PhD,[2] in his book *The Devil's Delusion,* lists the excess deaths that have occurred in the 20th century because of wars and tyrannical governments:

First World War (1914–18) . . . . 15 million
Russian Civil War (1917–22). . . . . 9 million
Soviet Union, Stalin's regime (1924–53) . . . . 20 million
Second World War (1937–45) . . . . 55 million
Chinese Civil War (1945–49) . . . . 2.5 million
People's Rep. of China, Mao
     Zedong's regime (1949–75). . . . . 40 million
Tibet (1950 et seq.) 600,000
Congo Free State (1886–1908) . . . . 8 million
Mexico (1910–20). . . . . 1 million
Turkish Massacres of Armenians
     (1915–23). . . . . 1.5 million
China (1917–28). 800,000
Korean War (1950–53) . . . . 2.8 million
North Korea (1948 et seq.) . . . . 2 million
Rwanda and Burundi (1959–95) . . . . 1.35 million
Second Indochina War (1960–75) . . . . 3.5 million
Ethiopia (1966–70). 400,000
Nigeria (1966–70). . . . . 1 million
Bangladesh (1971). . . . . 1.25 million
Cambodia, Khmer Rouge (1975–78). . . . . 1.65 million

---

2. Berlinski, David, b. 1942, PhD in philosophy from Princeton University, post-doctoral fellow in math and molecular biology at Columbia University, senior fellow at the Discovery Institute.

Mozambique (1975–91) . . . . 1 million

Afghanistan (1979–2001) . . . . 1.8 million

Iran-Iraq War (1980–88) . . . . 1 million

Sudan (1983 et seq.) . . . . 1.9 million

Kinshasa, DR Congo (1998 et seq.) . . . . 3.8 million

Philippines Insurgency (1899–1902) 220,000

Brazil (1900 et seq.) 500,000

Amazonia (1900–1912) 250,000

Portuguese Colonies (1900–1925) 325,000

French Colonies (1900–1940) 200,000

Japanese War (1904–5) 130,000

German East Africa (1905–7) 175,000

Libya (1911–31) 125,000

Balkan Wars (1912–13) 140,000

Greco-Turkish War (1919–22) 250,000

Spanish Civil War (1936–39) 365,000

Franco regime (1939–75) 100,000

Abyssinian conquest (1935–1941) 400,000

Finnish War (1939–40) 150,000

Greek Civil War (1943–49) 158,000

Yugoslavia, Tito's regime (1944–80) 200,000

First Indochina War (1945–54) 400,000

Columbia (1946–58) 200,000

India (1947) 500,000

Romania (1948–89) 150,000

Burma (Myanmar) (1948 et seq.) 130,000

Algeria (1954–62) 530,000

Sudan (1955–72) 500,000

Guatemala (1960–96) 200,000
Indonesia (1965–66) 400,000
Uganda, Idi Amin's regime (1972–79) 300,000
Vietnam, postwar Communist regime
    (1975 et seq.) 430,000
Angola (1975–2002) 550,000
East Timor, conquest by Indonesia
    (1975–99) 200,000
Lebanon (1975–90) 150,000
Cambodian Civil War (1978–91) 225,000
Iraq, Saddam Hussein's regime
    (1979–2003) 300,000
Uganda (1979–86) 300,000
Kurdistan (1980s, 1990s) 300,000
Liberia (1989–97) 150,000
Iraq (1990 et seq.) 350,000
Bosnia and Herzegovina (1992–95) 175.000
Somalia (1991 et seq.) 400,000

This is a shocking summation of mankind's inhumanity and a powerful negation* of those who believe the world is becoming a kinder and gentler place. Even a casual review of these statistics can easily be construed as a dilemma beyond the scope of human resolution. Admittedly, there is good in the world, but in no venue* does goodness stand alone in solitary victory. Always at the other end of the stick is the opposite, the potential of great evil.

This is also a physical world of structural division. Not only is the human psyche divided in a paradoxical conflict between strength and weakness; the physical world itself is composed of dynamic opposites. Physicists refer to this as broken symmetry.*

Even a perfect sphere, such as a billiard ball, demonstrates this when rotated around an axis, thus creating a north/south polarity. As mentioned earlier, when the poles are viewed toward each axis, the rotation at the top pole is turning clockwise while the bottom pole is turning counterclockwise. There is no change in the sphere's basic rotation. This polarization creates an existential reality of opposites such as east/west, north/south, right/left, up/down, forward/ backward, etc.

Humans disdain living in paradoxes* and attempt to solve the dilemmas they produce by choosing one side or the other. This tendency does not resolve the paradox but certainly sets the stage for differences, antagonism, conflict, wars, and attempted nihilism.* The hope in choosing one side or the other is that this action will defeat the paradox and establish stability and certainty for a peaceful life. Unfortunately, choosing one side over the other—no matter what the issue—does not resolve the paradox.

It's not unreasonable to expect an answer to the dilemma from within human understanding and experience. Historic cultures from ancient times until the present time clearly portray humankind's awareness of the dilemma and our myriad attempts to understand and treat the problem. Obviously, these efforts have not been successful since the Existential Dilemma still exists today. Nevertheless, the human mind is a clever problem solver and the historical search for an answer continues.

In the next two chapters I am exploring some of the precepts* of ancient religions and scanning some of the views of philosophy, psychology, and sociology* with their intention* of discovering a solution to the Existential Dilemma. At heart I'm an optimist, as was Ronald Reagan,[3] President of the United States in the 1980s. During his administration, several inter-party conflicts became chaotic. He was reported to have said in good humor, "With all this manure around here, there's got to be a pony somewhere."

So, let's look for the pony, shall we?

A Brief Survey of Proposed Religious Solutions

*"If we take the world's religions at their best,
we discover the distilled wisdom
of the human race."*
~HUSTON SMITH

Webster defines religion as "a set of beliefs concerning the cause, nature, and purpose of the universe, especially when considered as the creation of a superhuman agency or agencies, usually involving devotional and ritual observances, and often containing a moral code governing the conduct of human affairs."

Two ancient religions, Hinduism and Buddhism, recognized the forces of personal destruction surrounding life. To counteract

---

3. Reagan, Ronald, 1911–2004, American actor, politician; fortieth president of the United States; his speaking skills earned him the title "The Great Communicator."

these threats, preeminent* thinkers proposed concepts that guided mental attitudes and behaviors regarding successful living.

The first ancient religion we will survey is Hinduism.

Hinduism

Ancient Aryans invaded Northern India sometime after 2000 BC* and introduced Hinduism. The ultimate goal of Hinduism is the spiritual realization of one's inner identity with the divine absolute.* Over the centuries, the truths of the beliefs were written: the Hymns of the Veda (1400 to 800 BC), the Upanishads (800 BC), and the Bhagavad Gita (2nd century BC), the last of which is considered the book of excellence for the knowledge of truth.

Hinduism claims, "You can have what you want." Generally, people want four things in life: pleasure, worldly success, service or duty, and liberation. They want these infinitely unrestricted in terms of being, knowledge, and joy.

According to Hindu belief, the eternal* is buried deeply within the psyche, but certain conditions in life block us from reaching them, including mental and physical pain, ignorance, and restricted being. The resolution is to achieve the transcendent infinite state over the finite state. To attain this result, four pathways are proposed to unite the human spirit with God:

1. Knowledge—an intuitive discernment that turns the knower into that which he knows.
2. Love—directed toward God; the love that lies at the base of every heart.

3. Work—service and duty to God.
4. Yoga—a psychophysical* exercise that is "the royal road to reintegration,"* the "beyond that is within."

It seems ironic that Hinduism recognized that restriction of one's being is a deterrent* to attaining the absolute, and yet created the rigid caste system* of India. The dilemma remains! Let's look at another proposed religious solution.

Buddhism

The Buddha (Siddhartha Gautama)[4] was born in Nepal, raised in protected luxury, and was destined to fame and power. His father was a feudal king. While in his twenties, the young Siddartha became disillusioned about human suffering, disease, and death. At age 29, he left his wife and son and went into the forest for six years in search of enlightenment.* He experienced three phases of enlightenment: (1) learned yoga from Hindu masters, (2) joined a band of ascetics,* nearly dying from fasting, and (3) found the Middle Way.

The Buddha proclaimed, "Nirvana is the noble goal of life." He believed Nirvana* is the highest destiny of the human spirit, and its literal* meaning is extinction or nothing. This interpretation of "nothing" refers to what remains after the boundaries of finite life have been extinguished. Buddhism has no God, but rests on four noble truths of existence:

---

4. Gautama, Siddhartha, lived sometime in the 6th to 4th century AD; Indian philosopher, religious thinker, founder of Buddhism.

1. Suffering (life is dislocated)
2. Desire (for personal fulfillment)
3. Self-interest
4. The consuming power of cravings

According to Buddhist belief, these truths of life must be overcome. The way out of captivity is an eightfold path:

- ▶ Right views
- ▶ Right intent
- ▶ Right speech
- ▶ Right conduct
- ▶ Right livelihood
- ▶ Right effort
- ▶ Right mindfulness
- ▶ Right concentration

The Buddha, who died in 483 BC, was a profound thinker and teacher who didn't write anything. Over the centuries, however, his followers have written volumes.

In this brief assessment of the core beliefs of Hinduism and Buddhism, it is significant to note that any resolution of life's problems begins and ends with a person's knowledge, understanding, and effort. As insightful and noble as these concepts and precepts might be, the dilemma of existence remains unchanged.

In fact, it is reasonable to assume that the founders and followers of these religions recognized the ontological nature of the human dilemma. The chronic challenge was to divorce oneself from the intrinsic nature of a potentially corrupting reality and achieve a state of nothingness, as with Hinduism. Buddhism perhaps seeks a compromise with corruption and attempts to counteract its power by living with the goal of achieving perfection. What remains imperfect will gain opportunity to be hopefully overcome in the reincarnated* next life.

Another ancient religion, Judaism, separates itself from Hinduism and Buddhism in a significant way.

Judaism

Unlike Hinduism and Buddhism, Judaism is monotheistic,* proclaiming a God who created the universe and has a personal relationship to humans. Judaism recognizes mankind's estrangement* from God and God's loving outreach to humanity.

The origin of Judaism dates to about 2000 BC, in the final era of the Sumerian* culture. Born in the city of Ur, Abraham was chosen by God to be the father of a future great nation that would be a blessing to humanity. The Sumerians were polytheistic* as were almost all other religions of that era. Being monotheistic, Abraham was directed by God to emigrate to another location. Not knowing exactly where that place would be, he believed and trusted the promises of God and acted as directed by God. His faith became the foundation of the Jewish religion, a firm foundation based on Abraham's belief and faith.

The immediate descendants of Abraham experienced severe drought in the region of Canaan where they had settled, and were forced by famine to venture to Egypt. By unexpected circumstances, they found themselves living prosperously in Egypt's fertile land. Over the next 400 years, their population grew to several million. After the people were enslaved and brutalized by the pharaoh of Egypt, Moses led the Jewish people in a dramatic escape and they travelled back to Canaan (present day Israel and Palestine) in 1400 BC on a journey of over forty years. Along the way, God, through Moses, gave the people the Ten Commandments as their governing laws.

Human sacrifice ended with Abraham, but Judaism continued to be a sacrificial community. Animal and grain sacrifices provided "a pleasing odor" to the Lord, a guilt offering for the forgiveness of sins, and a reestablishment of a personal relationship with God. The Old Testament book of Leviticus thoroughly details these sacrificial ceremonies.

In order to understand the Hebrews' deeply felt need for sacrifice and atonement,* we need to look at Genesis, the first book of the both the Jewish and Christian scriptures. It strikes me as highly significant that Judaism understood the origin of the human dilemma, dating back to the first humans. Genesis 2:16-17 describes people's need for atonement. We read: "And the Lord God commanded the man, saying 'You may eat freely of every tree of the garden; but of the tree of knowledge of good and evil you shall not eat, for in the day that you eat of it you shall die.'"

Poetic expressions of reality and truth are commonly portrayed in the metaphors and allegories* of the scriptures. The ancient text from Genesis, quoted above, is one such allegory. Personal freedom is clearly recognized, but humans are commanded by God to avoid becoming enmeshed* in the bifurcated world of good and evil. Why? Because good and evil represent the physical domain with its polar opposites! Choosing, knowing, and experiencing the finite domain over the infinite means divorcing oneself from infinite consciousness, an act that chooses the finite over and against the infinite. Once the choice of the finite (the arena of time and space) is made, it becomes the point of no return because **the finite has no power to recapture the infinite**.

Judaism has failed to discover a remedy for the dilemma, but over the centuries it has prophesied the coming of a Messiah who would fulfill God's promise to Abraham that Israel would become a great nation. Judaism is still waiting for the Messiah.

In 70 AD, the Romans captured Jerusalem, the holy city of the Jewish people, and destroyed the city and the temple. Ever since then, the Jews have scattered all over the world and were without a national identity until 1948 when nationhood was granted to Israel. This action followed WWII, during which Germany slaughtered six million European Jews. At the present time, a large portion of the world population worships a God who sprang from Judaism around 610 AD (or a little later).

Islam

Islam traces its origin to Abraham, as do Judaism and Christianity. The difference is that Islam's genetic bloodline was developed through Abraham's second wife, Hagar, who was an Egyptian slave girl to Sarah, Abraham's first wife. Hagar gave birth to a son named Ishmael, who became the progenitor* of the Arab nations and future Islamic religion.

Islam worships Allah, "The God." The meaning of the word *Islam* is "peace and surrender." Muslims view God as the origin of their religion from "the beginning," and Mohammed as his prophet.

Born in 570 AD, Mohammed began experiencing revelations in about 610 AD and continuing for fifteen years. Mohammed, like the Buddha and Jesus, wrote nothing, but his small group of followers recorded his revelations.

Islam as a world religion began in 622 AD. Under persecution in Mecca, Mohammed moved to Medina, 280 miles north, then returned with an army and defeated those who opposed him at Mecca. He died in 632 AD, and by 700 AD, his army and followers had conquered Armenia, Persia, Syria, Palestine, Iraq, North Africa, and Spain. In 733 AD, the Islamic army was defeated in the Battle of Tours in France. If not for this defeat, all of Europe would have become Muslim.

Islam is founded on three principles: (1) there is one God, (2) God created the world and mankind, and (3) there will be a final judgment based on having lived in accordance with the will of God. Its holy book, the Koran (or Quran), is the "recitation" ("dictates of angels") and the guide to God's will.

According to the belief of Islam, each person is totally responsible for his or her relationship with God. There is no separation or estrangement from God; therefore, nothing stands between God and man. For Muslims, there is no Existential Dilemma! Under this belief system, the task of humans is to constantly strive to do God's will.

Islam views God as a God of mercy and compassion and sin as the failure to do God's will. To fulfill God's will, one must live in accordance with the five pillars:

1. Bear witness to Allah's saying, "There is no God but God, and Mohammed is his Messenger."
2. Pray five times a day in submission.
3. Give two and one-half percent to charity.
4. Fast when prescribed unless traveling, ill, or pregnant.
5. Make a pilgrimage to Mecca, if you are able, at least once in your life.

The Quest Continues

None of these world religions—Hinduism, Buddhism, Judaism, or Islam—can claim a resolution to the human dilemma. No human efforts have succeeded in dispelling the reality of death, the culprit of the dilemma and the crippler of a perfect life.

So then, if the ancients have failed to unravel the mystery, perhaps there is a relevant answer to be found in more recent ideas of philosophy, psychology, and sociology. Let's have a look at these next.

The Secular Quest

CHAPTER FIVE

The Search for a Solution in Philosophy, Psychology, and Sociology

*"Life is not a problem to be solved,
but a reality to be experienced."*
~SØREN KIERKEGAARD

Ever since Rene Descartes proposed the dichotomy* of mind and matter, philosophers have, by and large, developed their concepts around one side of the divide or the other. There are two schools of thought: some believe the essence of life is centered within the mind while others believe it centers on matter—a physical basis. Either way, paradoxical concepts are the outcome and no solution to the human dilemma appears imminent.

The history of philosophy begins around 400 BC in Greece where Aristotle,[1] Socrates,[2] and Plato[3] set the intellectual foundations for the following two thousand years. Philosophy surfaced and flourished with the Renaissance and the rise of academia. Is it possible that among these brilliant philosophers a solution to the dilemma may be discovered?

Many brilliant thinkers devoted their intellectual powers to unraveling the mystery of the dichotomy. They identified themselves as either idealists* or empiricists* and cleverly and convincingly presented their logic. Among those on the side of the **idealists** were Bishop George Berkeley,[4] Jean-Jacques Rousseau,[5] Immanuel Kant, Johann Fichte,[6] Arthur Schopenhauer,[7] Georg

---

1. Aristotle, 384–322 BC, Greek philosopher, scientist, and polymath in ancient Greece; a student of Plato.
2. Socrates, 470–399 BC, Greek Athenian philosopher; first moral philosopher of ethical tradition of thought; a founder of Western philosophy.
3. Plato, 424/423–348/347 BC, Athenian philosopher; founder of the Platonist school of thought and The Academy, the first Western institution of higher learning.
4. George Berkeley, 1685–1753, Anglo-Irish bishop, philosopher; his theory was "immaterialism," that ideas and mind are most important, and that material substances do not exist unless they are being perceived by minds.
5. Jean-Jacques Rousseau, 1712–1778, Genevan philosopher, writer, composer; his political philosophy influenced The Enlightenment and modern political, economic, and educational thought.
6. Johann Fichte, 1762–1814, German philosopher; a founding figure of German idealism; developed his idealism from the writings of Kant.
7. Arthur Schopenhauer, 1788–1850, idealist; advised overcoming the existential problems of the world with artistic, moral, and ascetic forms of awareness.

Hegel,[8] and Henri Bergson.[9] Among those on the side of **empiricism** were John Locke,[10] Benedictus Spinoza,[11] Thomas Hobbes,[12] Voltaire,[13] Gottfried Leibnitz,[14] and David Hume.[15]

Because I am searching for a possible solution to the Existential Dilemma, the division of philosophers into two camps reminds me that the polarization and bifurcation of human understanding confirms the reality of the dilemma. The elements of logic presented by each side appear to be rational and convincing. Unfortunately, their logic leaves only a paradoxical situation in its wake.

---

8. Georg Hegel, 1770–1831, German philosopher and idealist; one of the founding figures of Western philosophy; his influence extends to contemporary issues from aesthetics to ontology and politics.

9. Henri Bergson, 1859–1941, French philosopher known for his argument that processes of immediate experience and intuition are more significant than abstract rationalism and science for understanding reality.

10. John Locke, 1632–1704, English philosopher and physician; Enlightenment thinker known as the Father of Liberalism; one of the first British empiricists, following the tradition of Sir Thomas Bacon.

11. Benedictus Spinoza, 1632–1677, Dutch post-Cartesian philosopher and rationalist, definitive ethicist of the Dutch Golden Age; known for his magnum opus, *Ethics*.

12. Thomas Hobbes, 1588–1669, English philosopher; considered one of the founders of modern political philosophy; best known for his book *Leviathan*, in which he expounds social contract theory.

13. Voltaire, 1694–1778, French Enlightenment writer, historian, and philosopher; famous for wit, criticism of Christianity, as well as for his advocacy of free speech, freedom of religion, and separation of church and state.

14. Gottfried Leibnitz, 1646–1716, German polymath, mathematician, philosopher, scientist, and diplomat; wrote works on philosophy, theology, ethics, politics, law, history, and philology.

15. David Hume, 1711–1776, Scottish Enlightenment philosopher, historian, economist, librarian, and essayist; known for his influential system of philosophical empiricism, skepticism, and naturalism; examined the psychological basis of human nature.

The Mystery of the Origin of Knowledge

To briefly summarize the positions of the idealists and the empiricists, it appears their logic proceeds from the question *How does knowledge arise?* It was John Locke who argued that there is nothing in the mind except that which is first in the senses. According to Locke, all knowledge comes from experience that is dependent on the senses. The senses, in turn, are completely dependent upon matter, and therefore, matter must be the first cause.*

It was George Berkeley who first disagreed with Locke and used Locke's idea of the senses being dependent on matter as the point of departure. Berkeley proclaimed that matter does not exist except as a mental construct* and our knowledge of it is derived from the senses—a product of the mind. He dismissed empiricism and many agreed.

David Hume was 27 years younger than Berkeley and, at age 26, published his *Treatise on Human Nature*, considered to be one of the classics of modern philosophy. Hume proposed that the mind is known only as matter is known. Never is any such entity as the mind itself perceived.

Will Durant,[16] in his book *The Story of Philosophy*, summarizes the result of the bifurcation conflict quite concisely. The result was that Hume had apparently as effectually destroyed mind as Berkeley had destroyed matter. Nothing was left, and philosophy found itself in the midst of a ruin of its own origin. No wonder an

---

16. Will Durant, 1885–1981, American writer, historian, and philosopher, best known for co-authorship with his wife, Ariel, of the 11-volume *The Story of Civilization*.

God in the Quad

The Tree in the Quad

Bishop George Berkeley's ontological proof of the existence of God rested on the premise that things exist only insofar as they are perceived. A couple of centuries later, cleric Monsignor Ronald Knox produced the limerick that follows in support of Berkeley's philosophical stance:

> There was a young man who said, "God
> Must think it's exceedingly odd
> If He finds that this tree
> Continues to be
> When there's no one about in the Quad."

> *Reply*
>
> Dear Sir:
> Your astonishment's odd!
> I am always about in the Quad.
> And that's why the tree
> Continues to be,
> Since observed by
> Yours faithfully,
> GOD!

unidentified British wit advised abandonment of the controversy, saying, "No matter, never mind!"

German philosopher Georg Wilhelm Fredrick Hegel apparently believed he had resolved the dilemma. His method of analytic dialectic* recognized the bifurcation at play in the philosophical world and proposed a scheme of unification. He conceptualized reality as having two opposite values that he labeled "thesis" and "antithesis."* To these inherently partial concepts he offered what he believed was the greatest truth, the principle of "synthesis."* Presto, problem solved! Unification was achieved, or so he believed.

Karl Heinrich Marx[17] transposed* Hegel's concepts into the socioeconomic* realm, believing a classless society would solve the

---

17. Karl Heinrich Marx, 1813–1855, German philosopher, historian, sociologist, and revolutionary political theorist who published the Communist Manifesto with Friedrich Engels.

dilemma. Society would be "synthesized" into a single entity controlled by the government. History has recorded over and over the failure of single-party communism.* This supports the conclusion that philosophical thought does not have the power to resolve the Existential Dilemma.

Soren Kierkegaard[18] was intrigued with Hegel's concepts but found himself in total disagreement with Hegel's supposed solution. Kierkegaard's conclusion arrived with empty hands. He proclaimed no existential solution to the dilemma.

There is no philosophy or lifestyle capable of resolving the unsolved issues, so if this is the final truth of the matter, the human race has no choice but to "suck it up." Kierkegaard's followers created the current existential philosophy still prominent today. This philosophy is completely fatalistic and portrays a life that no has no exit except death. There is *no* exit!

However, if Kierkegaard is more completely understood, this is not his final answer. Kierkegaard concluded only that there was no *earthly* solution to the dilemma. He did not exclude other non-existential possibilities, such as life after physical death.

Existentialism* has not put to rest the debate surrounding the "mind-matter" question. In fact, the controversy rages on with great gusto on each side. Prominent in recent years were the four self-described "Brights": Richard Dawkins, Daniel Dennett, Sam Harris, and the late Christopher Hitchens. Each of them

---

18. Soren Kierkegaard, 1813–1855, Danish philosopher, theologian, poet, social critic, religious author; widely considered to be the first existentialist philosopher.

is a convinced atheistic materialist* and a popular writer. Their impact on current culture has been influential and dovetails with Newtonian classicism and Darwinian evolution. They represent a reality that is scientific and supported by physical evidence. It is Dennett who proclaims that consciousness does not exist, a belief shared by many empiricists and the other "Brights" who concluded that consciousness has no physical foundation, cannot be measured, and therefore has no reality. Their conclusion is that consciousness itself is merely an illusion.

Robert Lanza, MD, in his book *Beyond Biocentrism*,[19] takes the opposite viewpoint and states that the physical cosmos is an illusion.* Included in the illusion is death—it never happens! *Time* magazine in 2014 listed Lanza as one of the 100 most influential people in the world. In 2015, *Prospect* magazine named him one of the top 50 "world thinkers." I find his books intriguing, but I cannot share his concept of an illusionary cosmos. Humans are composed of both mind and body, intrinsically joined, and each is experienced as a reality. If a solution to the dilemma is to be found it must be inclusive of both sides of the dichotomy. It is convincingly clear that philosophy has failed and has itself become a product of the bifurcation.

---

19. R. P. Lanza and Bob Berman, *Beyond Biocentrism: Rethinking Time, Space, Consciousness, and the Illusion of Death* (BenBella Books, 2017).

At an Impasse

The truth is that we are living on a pile of slippery rocks. Nothing in the physical universe is permanent. We live in a world of beginnings and endings. All physical things change.

Science calls this "entropy"*—a process of decay and loss of material being. It would appear that the quest for a solution to the Existential Dilemma in the physical world realm has arrived at an emphatic answer: there is no answer! The dilemma lives within the subjective, transcendent consciousness as well as in physical reality, and any type of resolution must exert its power within the subjective, transcendent arena as well as in physical reality.

Perhaps this conclusion has been reached without adequate exploration. For millennia, the dilemma has been addressed by the most creative minds of many cultures, both east and west. The gurus* of Eastern religions, the philosophers of Western cultures, and more recent discoveries of scientists have all attempted to ease the struggles inherent in human experience.

Since the end of World War II (1945), strong ideational* efforts have been made to bring peace to the world. Perhaps the strongest of these efforts was the founding of the United Nations, a body of representatives of all nations. Since wars develop from conflicts between nations, it seemed completely logical to provide the opportunity for debate and discussion, and to activate reasonable solutions to problems. Sadly, wars and threats of war continue to plague the planet.

During the past few decades, Western nations have witnessed a concerted effort to create a one-world concept. To achieve this goal, all nations would dismantle their identity and their borders. A single world government would provide leadership, legal control, and economic and social justice. In the minds of these "globalists," the planet would become a unified kingdom, not a kingdom divided against itself. Would this eradicate the Existential Dilemma? Would this idea unify the foundational polarity of the cosmos? Emphatically, no!

Apparently, our quest for a solution to the Existential Dilemma has arrived at an impasse. We are abandoned at the end of the road in murky darkness with no apparent pathway out of the maze.

Let's review the building blocks leading to this conclusion, which we have examined in the previous chapters:

1. Since René Descartes, the divide between mind and body has prevailed in Western culture.
2. Humanity's views of materialism and science have evolved into the dominant view of reality.
3. In recent decades, the study of consciousness has arisen from dormancy. It remains a mystery to science.
4. For the purposes of this book, consciousness is viewed as transcendent, foundational, and universal.
5. Transcendent human consciousness faces constant threats, leaving people to worry that their conscious experience ends with the final destruction of temporal life.

It doesn't seem to me that the ancient men of renown in the fields of religion and philosophy have satisfactorily come up with a solution in spite of their sincerity, intense thoughtfulness, and wisdom.

Humpty Dumpty

"Humpty Dumpty sat on a wall
Humpty Dumpty had a great fall
All the King's horses and all the king's men
Couldn't put Humpty together again."
~Nursery Rhyme, Anonymous

Nursery rhymes frequently portray truths. This one clearly portrays the fact that the efforts of powerful people to "fix" things that are essentially irreparable fail to achieve the desired results.

Efforts of Psychology

Psychology is a study of the phenomenology* of the human mind and attempts to give a full description of the mental landscape. Its structure and methodology* are patterned to be a scientific model. Ever since the time of Sigmund Freud in the 1800s, psychology has flourished and expanded. It remains a popular subject today, with many psychologists devoting their careers to finding answers within a study of the human mind and how it works.

The success of chemistry and its atomic table were the inspiration for the development of a scientific model of the mind, and Sigmund Freud subsequently developed introspection* techniques to explore the unconscious and repressed aspects of awareness. He believed the cause of the mind's pathology* lay deep in forgotten experiences within the recesses of the mind.

Out of this belief system, psychoanalysis* was born, with the promise of a consciousness freed from neurosis and psychosis.* The pundits* of society in Europe and the United States glommed onto its discoveries as brilliant revelations long hidden from the world. However, from the 1930s through the 1950s, psychoanalysis gradually slipped into disfavor because it was expensive and out of reach for most people, but more importantly, it really didn't fulfill its promise. It failed the "scientific" test because research exhibited no consistency and therefore no reliability.

Undeterred by this outcome, psychology turned its attention away from introspection of the psyche toward observable, measurable behavior. Based on Ivan Pavlov's stimulus-response* research on dogs, John B. Watson and B. F. Skinner developed the theory of Behaviorism.* Human behavior and mental functioning were viewed as reflex activities founded upon the mechanistic principles of stimulus-response. According to this theory, the human race was the product of a deterministic* universe, and humans' private experiences of personhood became psychological fiction. Popular in the 1960s, behavior modification as a therapy technique designed to negate* behavioral pathology failed to deliver consistently positive results.

During the 1970s, many therapy styles arose such as Transactional Analysis,* Cognitive Therapy,* and Client-Centered Therapy,* each focusing on the life experiences of individual persons. Also, during the 1970s, a major development occurred with the discovery of psychoactive* drugs. Pharmaceutical research developed medications that could alter brain function and counter the effects of anxiety, depression, and psychotic episodes. Consequently, psychiatry and other medical professions now rely heavily on drug treatments.

Overall, the profession of psychology has been beneficial to society in many ways. Its therapies have been helpful to countless numbers of people experiencing mental and emotional conflicts. The scientific approach in exploring the psyche has revealed extensive knowledge of the brain and its function. The testing and measurement of mental ideation and factors of intelligence etc. have proven useful.

However, the inability to comprehend consciousness has limited psychology's full understanding of the human psyche. Using only the scientific, objective framework limits the possibility of understanding the subjective reality of consciousness. Working with "half a deck," psychology has not found a solution to the Existential Dilemma.

Perhaps a solution can be found by the establishment of methods to control the behavior of large groups of people. These efforts are usually grouped under the large umbrella of sociology.

The Efforts of Sociology

Sociology is the study or science of the origin, development, organization, and functioning of human society. It discovers and examines the fundamental laws of community organization. From this body of conceptual knowledge have emerged professions such as social work, urban planning, governmental public support programs, community organizations, and social justice movements.

Sociology concerns itself with the exigencies* of existence and can profoundly influence events from the local community up to the international scene. As mentioned earlier, during the past few decades, Western nations have witnessed a concerted globalist effort to create a one-world government, with the aim of nations eventually dismantling their sovereign* borders and dissolving their individual identities. The European Union (EU), currently centered in Brussels, Belgium, was designed to begin the process of implementing this plan—with open borders, socialist equalizing theories,* and increasing government control.

Should this effort someday succeed, would it eradicate the polarities and dichotomies of existence? Would people finally live in unity and peace? As history marches on, we sadly can conclude: no.

In this chapter and the two preceding it, I have briefly surveyed elements of a few of the great religions of antiquity and elements of 400 years of philosophy, psychology, and sociology and their efforts. So, where does that leave us in our quest?

Ronald Reagan's optimism has not carried the day; manure abounds; no pony is found! The tragedy of the Existential Dilemma continues on generation after generation with no solution.

As the once-prominent American vocalist Peggy Lee[20] used to sing, "Is this all there is?"

---

20. Peggy Lee, 1920–2002, born Deloris Engstrom; American jazz, popular music singer, composer, and actress over a career spanning seven decades.

So . . . How Shall We Live?

CHAPTER SIX

Living with the Existential Dilemma

"Out, out, brief candle! Life's but a walking
shadow, a poor player that struts and frets
his hour upon the stage and then is heard
no more. It is a tale told by an idiot,* full
of sound and fury, signifying nothing."
~WILLIAM SHAKESPEARE,[1]
MACBETH

In the early days of television, a popular actor named William Bendix* portrayed a loveable, simple family man in a series known as *The Life of Riley*. In response to his innumerable fixes and predicaments, his memorable cry of frustration in each episode was, "What a revolting development this has turned out to be."

---

1. William Shakespeare, Shane Barnes, and Aidan Coleman, "Act Five," in *William Shakespeare's Macbeth* (Insight Publications, 2017).

I'm sure Mr. Bendix would find a strong affinity with the dilemmas presented in the previous chapters and also with what follows in this one. The Existential Dilemma has not been resolved, and, as persons living in this world, we apparently have to make the best of it. How do we humans live in this polarized and paradoxical world?

The philosophy called existentialism clearly portrays the human race as encapsulated in a futile dilemma with no escape. Søren Kierkegaard, the Danish theologian, philosopher, and prolific author of dozens of books, is considered to be the father of this philosophy. In his writings, he strongly emphasized paradoxical structures of reality, which have been influential in my concept of the Existential Dilemma. Although Kierkegaard developed the concepts of existentialism, he actually did not identify himself as an existentialist. Even though he was a severe critic of the Danish Lutheran Church, he championed the Christian message that the opposite of sin is not virtue, but faith! Two of his books, *The Sickness unto Death* and *The Concept of Anxiety*, have been instrumental in the unfolding themes of my thesis.

We have discovered that all of the thinking and proposals of great minds have not solved the dilemma, so how do we live with it? Obviously, since we're alive, we do live with it. In fact, any overall survey of the social culture of most Western nations reveals a complex infrastructure* created to mitigate* the effects of the Existential Dilemma and serve the needs of citizens from womb to tomb.

How We Live with the Dilemma

Governments, institutions, and corporations, along with myriad private enterprises, are the instruments that attempt to make collective life livable. They provide protections and supports to help counteract ever-present threats to human existence. Behind this scenario are the multitudes who live with the Existential Dilemma 24/7. As previously noted, each individual person in this multitude has an underlying consciousness that is both strong and weak. The interplay* of strengths and weaknesses dynamically undermines the psyche of each individual human being on earth.

The paradoxical strength and weakness of the human psyche plays a dynamic role not only in the everyday life of each person, but also specifically in the formation of political theory and the creation of governments. Democratic and conservative governments favor a governing style that allows more freedom and requires more personal responsibility of those who are governed. They lean toward the side of personal strength. Communist and socialist* governments tend to lean toward the weakness side and view society as needing more authority over and control of its citizens. Freedom in this type of system is more limited. Each political body functions within the polarized/paradoxical sphere and each believes it has the best-coping philosophy to manage the Existential Dilemma. Both systems represent a degree of truth, but neither has the final answer to the dilemma; they are subjected to the overriding dominance of inherent paradoxical reality.

In addition to the efforts of governments, the efforts of religion and philosophy and the mental health professions of psychiatry, psychology, and sociology have developed over the past century or more in order to provide understanding of and methods to cope with mental and social pathology. The success of these professions, though noble in their esteem of the person, has fallen short of expectations. Reasons vary, of course, but a major problem occurs when these professions identify exclusively with science. A human being is both mind and body. By this definition the category of metaphysics must play a role in searching for solutions because metaphysics incorporates both the mind and the body.

Another problem arises with the assumption that humans are perfectible and are capable of creating a utopian society. This philosophy is confined to the potential of humanity to resolve its dilemmas. The assumption is that deviations from "normalcy" can be corrected through intervention and therapy.

In this approach the missing component is consciousness, in which the origin of the Existential Dilemma is embedded. Without the inclusion of consciousness there is a limited understanding of the pathology involved. Proponents of this philosophy view the underlying ontological anxiety as a tagalong symptom of the pathology rather than its cause. In this book, I am asserting that the cause of pathology with its destructive outcomes resides *within* the Existential Dilemma, where the powers of disunity and anxiety permeate all reality.

What the Existential Dilemma Looks Like

I have emphasized the undermining of human strength by anxiety as a primary cause of human dysfunction.* Although compromised, the strength of consciousness remains a viable force for good. Evil (which is real) challenges good every step of the way, but the principles of reason, altruism, honesty, and goodwill still demonstrate strength, and institutions within society certainly can promote the good as well.

To portray the nature of living with the Existential Dilemma is a formidable challenge. No two persons are alike, and the world in which we live is not static, but saturated with perpetual change. I have created a dimensional graph to illustrate the universality of the Existential Dilemma, using a vertical and a horizontal axis to illustrate this scenario within the Existential Dilemma. The graph affords a generalized overview of the populace in all societies of the world and the formations of societal groupings within the determinants of the graph.

On the following page you will find a two-dimensional graph with a vertical (north-south) and a horizontal (east-west) axis. Each axis is a polarized measurement of opposite traits. In the narrative that follows, these traits are presented as expressions and choices of individuals.

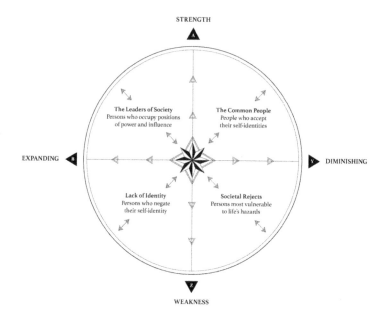

Living with the Existential Dilemma

The **vertical axis** represents a person who demonstrates the strengths and weaknesses of existence. The **horizontal axis** represents the reality in which the person lives in an expanded* or limited lifestyle in the time/space world. Each of the axes exhibits the paradoxical possibilities of living in the world of opposites. Together, the axes symbolize the person and the reality of human existence. Outward movement in any direction from the center signifies the increasing intensity of the traits. A person can move any direction as influenced by their talents, experience, and degree of ontological anxiety.

The vertical axis on the graph is labeled AZ, pertaining to individual strengths and weaknesses. The horizontal axis is labeled BY, pertaining to increasing and decreasing lifestyles. Notice that the crossing of the axes creates four quartiles. Each quartile represents a quality of character traits and lifestyle varieties.

The concept of the graph is to illustrate how humans live in the Existential Dilemma with its polarity, diversity, and human anxiety. The quartiles in this graph are superimposed on the open, inclusive frame of reality. This creates the possibility of specific groupings and trait descriptions. It positions the masses of the general population into the quartile that depicts the traits that tend to predominate and differentiate* between the quartiles. I have listed some of the personality traits and coping mechanisms found in each quartile.

Within the AB quartile are the leaders of society, those who occupy positions of power and influence. These are people who demonstrate strength in their personal lives and choose to live an expanding lifestyle by applying their intelligence and talents to achieve prominence. Many may have dominant personalities, high self-esteem, and confidence. They are educated, knowledgeable, responsible, and willing to take risks. Wealth and influence may add to their persona.

Who are these people? At the pinnacle are the world leaders, presidents, prime ministers, and dictators of nations. A long list would include famous philosophers, authors, leaders of science, medicine, religion, industry, and persons of great personal wealth. In the United States they include military leaders, the

CEOs of large corporations, congressional leaders, famous artists, entertainers, Supreme Court justices, coaches, and top athletes. At the state/city levels are the governors, mayors, and elected officials who represent the primary levels of society. The persons represented in this quartile strongly influence each of the other three quartiles.

The AY quartile identifies those designated as the common people who accept their self-identities. They are less interested in becoming famous than in establishing a secure and meaningful lifestyle. They are typically responsible, reliable, and law-abiding citizens. The moral-ethical values of society are integrated into their lifestyles. Qualities of being industrious, success-oriented, and living with moderation and balance are basic. This designates the middle class with its strong family values, community orientation, and willingness to be contributors to and supporters of the general good of society.

Who are these people? They are the farmers, factory workers, teachers, lawyers, doctors, entrepreneurs, firemen, policemen, and homemakers, among others. These are the persons who occupy and maintain the very foundations of society. This quartile represents the largest group of the population. These individuals tend to experience anxiety at a lower level than those in the other three quartiles, possibly because of consistent social patterns, traditions, and group identities that people in this quartile tend to sustain.

The BZ quartile portrays persons who tend to negate their self-identity for reasons that may be obscure. However, they value their lifestyle and can become prominent social figures. These persons can be emotionally sensitive and potentially fragile. This sets the stage for experiencing higher levels of existential anxiety and can become the motive for compensating lifestyle choices. These persons are imaginative, creative, possessors of strong desires, and often may become well-known personalities. Their underlying self-doubts remain the motive for achievement and can undermine personal stability. Other personality traits may include self-centered preoccupation, attention seeking, contrived behaviors, addictive* tendencies, and the manipulation of others.

Who are these persons? Many are audience seekers who relish the attention and approval of admirers. These may include movie and television actors who make their living assuming many identities. In this quartile are the "wannabes" and "could-have-beens." They may also include the social climbers and the addictive personalities. It's possible that some are content being incognito* and living a quiet lifestyle—not too expansive, but comfortable.

The YZ quartile identifies persons most vulnerable to the hazards of life. Many are cast into this category through no fault of their own. The physically and mentally handicapped are examples. Some in this quartile were reared in dysfunctional and rejecting families. Generally, these are dependent persons, followers, with lower self-esteem and fewer coping skills. Finding life a losing proposition, many are corralled into an escapist lifestyle.

Sociopathic and psychopathic* developments frequently follow this escapist mindset. Mental depression can lead to feelings of despair and hopelessness, which in turn can trigger hostility and violence. Many commit criminal acts. Perhaps the majority of them seek ways of passively accepting what life has dealt them and accept support from the public dole.

Some, of course, are minimally employed and self-supporting, but choose a hermit lifestyle. (It must be noted that there is an exception here: many handicapped people, whether their handicap is genetic or situational, have risen above their circumstances and become inspirations to those of us who have been more fortunate.)

Who are these people? They may be chronic welfare recipients, the mentally ill, the homeless, criminals, prison inmates, and those needing the support and protection of society. Generally, these are often considered to be "losers" in the game of life. Often they are neglected and forgotten by society.

I also must note here that human beings are very complex creatures and the graph is merely indicative of the power of the dilemma. It is not meant to be a confining, limiting description of human beings, but merely an indicator of how we humans attempt individually to cope with the fix we find ourselves in. No one escapes!

Enter the Findings of Quantum Physics

Living with the Existential Dilemma is indeed a challenge for humanity. The prevailing odds against living a life of meaning and purpose appear to be overwhelming. But I am stunned to observe the resilience,* hopefulness, and creativity within the souls of people. What is the pervasive dynamic that empowers the minds of human beings to persevere in their quest for understanding the mysteries of life? From whence cometh hopefulness?

To this point, so far, I have presented transcendent consciousness as potentially possessing this power. From this evolving mindset have flowed the marvelous discoveries of science that must now include the mind-boggling findings of quantum physics. The worldview of Newtonian determinism has been foundationally overturned. Science itself has illustrated the inadequacy of humanistic materialism to present the entire truth of reality.

My purpose in writing this book has been to propose an answer to the unresolvable Existential Dilemma, and I believe it is partially found in the emerging field of quantum physics. Helping the reader gain a rudimentary* knowledge of quantum physics and its enigma will be helpful in gaining an understanding of how I arrived at my thesis. Getting to the destination is half the fun. So, let us push optimistically onward.

The Thinker

CHAPTER SEVEN

The Quantum Enigma

*"I think that I can safely say that nobody
understands quantum mechanics."*
~RICHARD FEYNMAN[1]

The year is 1801 in England. Thomas Young, a twenty-eight-
year-old physician who was a child prodigy, has released a
pamphlet defending his disagreement with Isaac Newton's theory
of light particles. Young is best described as a polymath,* a person
of great learning in several fields of study. Born in 1773, the oldest
of ten children, he was reading fluently at age two and had read
the entire Bible twice by age six. He spoke more than 12 languages
and was instrumental in deciphering Egyptian hieroglyphics.*

Young's interest in the transmission of light led to the creation
of a measurement device demonstrating a proven fact—the nature
of light is a wave. This device projected a beam of light through two
screens, the first with a single slit and the second with two slits. As the

---

1. Richard P. Feynman, *The Character of Physical Law* (Cambridge, MA, etc.:
M.I.T. Press, 1990).

light penetrated the two screens through the slits, the ensuing light pattern focused on a third screen, revealing a diffraction* pattern that clearly demonstrated the wave nature of light. The waves interfered with each other, creating crests and troughs like waves on the surface of water. This procedure is now known as the double-slit experiment and is common in high school and college physics classes.

Even before Young, Christian Huygens had questioned Newton's particle theories of light by demonstrating that two colliding beams of light produced no particles. Newton had experimented with light and was aware of the idea of light waves* but viewed diffraction as the result of "forces" acting on light particles and had determined that the wave* could not be the fundamental nature of light. Given the seeming impossibility of the task it is surprising, even shocking, to learn of the discoveries which are now referred to as quantum mechanics.

Young's pamphlet sold only one copy. He was viciously attacked for challenging Newton. But, as history reveals, this was the beginning of the end for Newton's particle theory.

Wave/Particle Duality*

Almost like a phantom,* the enigma of quantum mechanics stole into the area of science. Another 100 years elapsed before the dawn of the seemingly absurd notion that particles could also be waves. This duality remains a mystery and has challenged the intelligence of the brightest and best of humanity.

The purpose of this chapter is to bring to our awareness the nature of the microcosm and its revolutionary influence over the

Newtonian classical interpretation of the macrocosm.* We will spend time looking at some of the enigmatic aspects of quantum understanding, and I make no presumption of fully assessing quantum theory.* The Technik Museum in Berlin states:

> *"Earlier in human history, it was not possible to observe the world of very small things—the microcosm—or the world of the very large things—the macrocosm. People could only apprehend a small portion of their environment: the portion they could perceive with their unaided senses.*
>
> *"Devices like the microscope or the laser make it possible for people to expand their world of experience and peer into the world of the tiniest things. This has given us insight into the makeup of human cells and matter.*
>
> *"Modern science shows us that different laws apply in the microcosm than we immediately perceive. Especially in physics, traditional views about atoms, particles, and light turned out **not** to be valid. They have been since been replaced by new models—models that exceed the bounds of human imagination."[2]*

In this book, I have used the word "microcosm" to describe the very tiny subatomic scales where quantum interactions dominate. The word "macrocosm" is used to describe the large world of visible matter and the cosmos beyond.

Since 1801, the knowledge of the microcosm has grown exponentially, but at a snail's pace. The intellectual challenges to

---

2. Technik Museum, Berlin.

understanding the microcosm have been so profound that even generations of physicists have not discovered absolute answers. These men of science can be portrayed as an array of blind men attempting to piece together a gigantic, complicated jigsaw puzzle.

A brief overview of the basics of quantum structure* will introduce the enigma that science itself has discovered in the quantum realm.* The determinism of Newtonian classical physics has now been replaced by a concept of probabilities underlying all physical reality. The wave/particle duality demonstrates the essence of the quantum enigma. How is it possible for a "solid" nugget of material, the particle, to originate from a source "waving" in space?

In 1905, Albert Einstein published his Theory of Special Relativity,* which applied to all physical phenomena in the absence of gravity. This astounded a world that believed time and space were absolute and unchanging. Then, in 1915, he published his Theory of General Relativity, which explains the law of gravitation and its relationship to other forces of nature, applying to both the cosmological and astrophysical* realms. These two theories superseded* the theories of Isaac Newton and transformed theoretical physics and astronomy in the 20th century.

The theories forced the revision of Newton's concept of time, space, and gravity. Scientists no longer viewed the cosmos as permanently fixed, but completely open to influences of momentum, space, mass, and gravity. Further experiments verified that matter influences space, and altered space tells matter how to move. Time and space, the domain of human existence, can no longer be perceived as fixed absolutes. The very foundations of physical realty have been cast into the arena of relativity. It appears to me that the anchor of humanistic materialism has been lost in a sea of uncertainty.

Any reference to Einstein brings to mind his world-famous equation, "E=MC squared," in which E (energy) is equated with M (mass) times the square of the speed of light. He came to this understanding quite casually and intuitively in 1905 while developing insights on relativity. The quote below is from a letter written by Einstein to a colleague, Conrad Habicht, in 1905:

> *"One more consequence of the electrodynamics* paper has also crossed my mind. Namely, the relativity principle, together with Maxwell's equations,* requires that mass be a direct measure of the energy contained in a body. Light carries mass with it. With the case of radium* there should be a noticeable reduction of mass. The thought is amusing and seductive; but for all I know, the good Lord might be laughing at the whole matter and might have been leading me up the garden path."*[3]

The discovery of the equivalence of energy and matter was literally quite earthshaking, as it led to the development of the atomic bomb in World War II. Perhaps more significant was the revelation that the "solidarity"* of all matter in the cosmos was equal to the mystery of unseen energy. E=MC squared becomes another quantum enigma along with the wave/particle enigma.

---

3. Albert Einstein and John J. Stachel, *The Collected Papers of Albert Einstein* (Princeton, NJ: Princeton University Press, 1987).

Quantum mechanics is so enigmatic to our common everyday view of how the world works that it can create an emotional longing to forget the quantum and stay put with Newton's determinism. But, alas, quantum theory has never failed to be accurate in its discoveries and predictions. One third of the US economy is now based on products developed from quantum theory. Included among these products are the MRI, television, microwave appliances, and mobile phones, to name just a few of them.

Again, the intent of this chapter is to introduce quantum concepts that defy common reasoning and to set the stage for the chapters that are to follow, which will describe reality in a different mode from that of the polarization of materialism. The wave/particle enigma has been introduced, and what follows will be an abbreviated presentation of the structure of particles, forces, the atom,* nonlocality,* and the uncertainty principle.*

As previously mentioned in Chapter Two, science has discovered four forces that govern the cosmos. They are the electromagnetic force, gravity, the strong force, and the weak force. Each of the four forces emanates from its own individual field and is spread out in space over the entire cosmos.

Quantum scientists theorize that the fields of these forces contain waves, or vibrations, of potential energy not yet formed into particles. These vibrations—when agitated, accelerated, or disturbed, even by consciousness—will coalesce* into bundles of energy. This energy is the foundation of what is referred to as a particle. When physicists do experiments with the particles, they "coax" the wave function to "collapse" into a particle, which they can then measure by instruments such as a Geiger counter.*

Two general types of particles have been identified, labeled bosons and fermions.* Bosons are the particles that carry the forces. Fermions are the particles that make up matter. The differences between them are distinct. Bosons take up no space and millions of them can pile up on each other at the same location. Thus, they can combine to create a macroscopic force field. Fermions take up space and no two can occupy the same location. This is why collections of fermions make up objects like tables, chairs, the moon and galaxies. As mentioned in Chapter Two, it is the Higgs boson that creates mass (collections of particle energy) and matter.

The Electromagnetic Force

The electromagnetic force is propagated in a continuous span of wavelengths ranging from a tiny fraction of the size of an atom to longer than the size of the universe in their waviness. Science has formalized them into the electromagnetic spectrum, classified into eight ranges of radiation. Beginning with high-energy short wavelengths, they are:

1. gamma rays*
2. X-rays*
3. ultraviolet light (UV)*
4. visible light*
5. infrared light*
6. terahertz rays*
7. microwaves*
8. radio waves

The first three wavelengths are potentially destructive to the DNA in the human genome* but are filtered to essentially safe levels in the atmosphere. The remaining five wavelengths are increasingly long, lower in energy, and therefore safer.

The harnessing of the electromagnetic force has revolutionized life on Earth. Imagine, if you can, a world without electricity. And yet, this is exactly the reality my immigrant grandparents experienced upon arriving in the United States 150 years ago. It was a world of kerosene lamps, horse power, and handicraft; clothing and tools were often made at home. The industrial revolution generated by the discovery of electric power has been something to behold.

The Gravitational Force

The gravitational force* is very familiar to all of us. This is the force that keeps us from flying off into space. It also causes the earth to rotate around the sun and the moon to rotate around the earth. The gravitation particle has yet to be discovered, but obviously it must exist. Science seems to be in no hurry to locate it, probably because its function is so well understood. Its discovery probably wouldn't even win a Nobel Prize.

The Strong Force

To describe the strong force, some understanding of the atom is needed. I will use a simplified model of the atom to make this topic more accessible to readers.

Since the time of the Greek philosopher Democritus, who first proposed the concept of the existence of the atom, it was believed the atom was the basic, indestructible unit of all matter. In 1964, Murray Gell-Mann, among others, discovered quarks,* which compose the substance of the nucleus* of the atom.

The nucleus is made of protons* and neutrons around which rotate electrons.* It is the quarks that bind the nucleus together under the control of the strong force. The quarks are the particles that comprise the protons and neutrons, and they in turn are bound by particles called gluons.* The electrons, however, are not bound to the nucleus permanently, but can jump around between discrete energy levels while circling the nucleus.

The strong force is the strongest of the four forces. It is responsible for keeping quarks locked inside protons and neutrons crammed inside the atomic nucleus.

The Weak Force

The weak force is identified as the force that mediates* the radioactive decay* of particles. This process of decay is occurring constantly throughout space among the force fields.

The Higgs boson has been identified as a product of the weak force and therefore is governed by it. Mass and matter formation are the result of the creation process of particle decay, which the Higgs boson filters down to the elementary particles. The bosons—or carriers of the weak force—were identified in the 1960s by physicist Steven Weinberg.

There are three force elements identified as W+, W-, and Z. The complexity of these quantum qualities exceeds the need of description in this short thesis. Volumes about this topic have been written by Nobel Prize winners if the reader wishes to gain more understanding.

The Influence of Consciousness

I have mentioned that consciousness is an influential cause of the wave collapse into the formation of particles. How can this be? Let's take some time to unpack this interesting reality. How can consciousness possibly be connected to the process of creating the physical world?

Bruce Rosenblum and Fred Kuttner, in the book *Quantum Enigma*, state the following:

> *"Consciousness and the quantum enigma are not just two mysteries;* **they are the two mysteries***. The first, the experimental demonstration of the quantum enigma, presents us with the mystery of the objective physical world 'out there,' and the second presents us with the mystery of the subjective, mental world 'in here.' quantum mechanics appears to connect the two."*[4]

If human consciousness is not enough of a mystery in its own right, we are now introduced to another enigma: the dynamic role

---

4. Fred Kuttner and Bruce Rosenblum, *Quantum Enigma: Physics Encounters Consciousness, Second Edition* (Oxford University Press, USA, 2011).

consciousness plays within the time/space physical world. Since 1927, the Copenhagen interpretation* of quantum physics has supported this enigmatic position as standard. As expected, there are extremists on both sides of the dilemma. There are those who proclaim consciousness doesn't exist and those who proclaim the physical world is an illusion. Either way, consciousness is the enigma.

Could it be that consciousness is "The Theory of Everything," the ultimate quest of quantum physics?

The Uncertainty Principle

In May 1927, Werner Heisenberg introduced the uncertainty principle.* This insertion of uncertainty into the fabric of quantum mechanics was the final nail in the coffin of Newton's clockwork universe. The certainty of classical physics has had to step aside and acknowledge that physical reality is composed of quantum uncertainty. This uncertainty factor became evident when attempts were made to measure the wave/particle phenomenon.

Particles have two qualities that cannot be measured simultaneously: location and velocity. The more accurately you measure an object's position, the more uncertain you will be about its speed. This principle—the wave/particle duality concept—presents a mental conundrum* to human perception. A particle is a composite of each quality, and when the wave aspect is observed it presents itself in the form of a tangible, measurable physical object. This can be metaphorically described as two sides of the same coin; the two aspects are a unified duality and viewed as complementary* to each other.

Again, when observed, the particle form has two qualities (location and momentum), but they can only be measured separately. The result is an uncertainty and a probability. To measure one entity disturbs the other and vice versa.

Nonlocality

Classic Newtonian physics informs us that all action, motion, or physical change occurs locally. For example, the cue ball on the billiard table strikes the rack of balls and scatters them in many directions. The cause and its effect happen at one location and are beyond debate.

However, quantum physics presents another enigma. At the quantum level (wave/particle), every entity is interconnected. After decades of theoretical debate, the issue was experimentally tested and confirmed, as the technology had finally become available to create measuring devices capable of handling the experiments. In 1982, Alain Aspect and his colleagues at the University of Paris published the results of their research. Aspect's experiments measured correlation between pairs of photons. The particles were separated and were far enough apart to preclude any causal or local connections. No correlation was possible unless the causation acted faster than the speed of light. In other words, instantaneously! It did—and correlation was established!

Aspect's conclusions were confirmed in 1997 by Nicolas Gisin and his colleagues at the University of Geneva. This team created pairs of entangled* photons and dispatched them through fiber-optic lines to two Swiss villages. The distance between Belleview and Berne is 11 kilometers or nearly seven miles. In the quantum world this distance is comparable to conducting the experiment with light-years of separation between the particles. Each photon of the pair seemed to "know" what measurement had been made on its distant partner and to respond in like manner. Instantly! Einstein referred to this as "spooky action at a distance." Nonlocality has been affirmed, which means that the cosmos is interconnected at the foundation of its particle reality. Is it universal consciousness that is creating the "knowing" interconnectedness? Whatever it is, it is mind-blowing.

Two hundred years have elapsed since science became interested in pursuing knowledge of the microcosm. In the past 100 years, there have been great strides taken in this field, but the discoveries have proved to be so confounding that they defy common understanding. For this reason, the general populations of the world have largely ignored quantum realities. While mysteries attract some inquiring minds, others find the mystery so daunting that they avoid the subject altogether.

My central focus in this book has been on the Existential Dilemma that engulfs all humanity. This too remains a mystery and an enigma. My purpose for including a chapter on the quantum enigma is to establish and emphasize and the fact that *ultimate reality* is *not* to be found in the structure of the physical domain. This also is true as it pertains to the Existential Dilemma. No solution has been discovered in the physical realm that mitigates or obliterates* the anxiety of the dilemma and its final cause, namely death. However, I wish to note and emphasize that both the *quantum* and the *dilemma* feature *consciousness* as an overriding principle.

As our search for an answer to the Existential Dilemma continues in the following chapters, consciousness will play a major role.

Given for You, Luke 22:19

CHAPTER EIGHT

The Jesus Enigma

"In this world you have tribulation: but be
of good cheer, I have overcome the world."
~JOHN 16:33B, KJV

The Existential Dilemma has not been resolved; the world has languished in its clutches since the beginning of time. Over the centuries, many creative coping concepts have been proposed but none of them have demonstrated the power needed to release the stranglehold of the dilemma on humanity. The crisis continues to this very day. Is there no choice remaining but to wave the white flag of surrender to this Gordian knot? Is the dilemma totally and permanently impossible to overcome?* (Note: "Gordian knot" is an expression used to describe a seemingly unsolvable or difficult-to-solve problem.)

Gordian Knot

According to legend, Alexander the Great[1] came upon an oxcart that was fastened with a virtually intractable knot to a pole at the entrance of a city. It was said that whoever could untangle the knot would become the master of all Asia. After trying unsuccessfully to untangle the knot, Alexander took his sword and simply cut it off. (He later became the master of all Asia!)

But back to the question: Is the dilemma totally and permanently intractable? From the perspective of a rational mind, the answer must be "Yes!" The ontological, intrinsic, and systemic* nature of the problem confirms this position. An apt example is the inability of any person to lift himself by his own bootstraps. Obviously true!

---

1. Alexander the Great, 356 BC to 323 BC, king of the Greek kingdom of Macedonia; taught by Aristotle, overthrew the Persian empire and laid the foundation for the Hellenistic world of territorial kingdoms.

Over the course of human history, there has only been one person who has risen to successfully challenge the Existential Dilemma. That person is Jesus of Nazareth. He is the most enigmatic person to have ever walked the earth, and from him comes the most profound* message of all time. He spoke it simply: "He who has ears to hear, let him hear" (Matthew 11:15). What he said he would do, he did, and his actions spoke even more emphatically than his words. How his life, death, and resurrection impact the Existential Dilemma is the subject of this chapter.

The Historic Jesus

Jesus was born approximately two thousand years ago in Palestine, which at that time was a remote Jewish province under Roman administration. He was of Jewish descent and was of the house and family of King David, of the tribe of Judah. First-century AD writings of each of the historians Suetonius, Tacitus, and Josephus mention him only briefly. Jesus himself left no written record, but the New Testament reveals all that is known about his personhood, message, and life. Born in humble circumstances and executed as a criminal by the Romans at a relatively young age (33), we might expect such a person would certainly be forgotten and any records about him deposited in the dustbin of history. Obviously, that has not been the case.

Over the course of just three years, Jesus traveled throughout the provinces of Israel—Galilee, Samaria, and Judea—proclaiming the arrival of the kingdom of God. He presented his message with ultimate authority, and his mission attracted throngs of followers wherever he went. On occasion, he ministered, preached, and lectured to thousands in open arenas. Many were miraculously healed and set free from demonic oppression.

Jesus' local fame became so prominent and extensive that the common people clamored to make him their king. The chief priests and Pharisees (the intelligentsia of their day) became alarmed at this prospect and plotted to end his life. The Sanhedrin (the Jewish court of law) brought a charge of blasphemy against Jesus, condemning him to death by crucifixion. Every procedural rule was violated in accomplishing this judgment. Jesus' ignominious* death would bring certain and final closure to his mission, or so the religious leaders assumed.

How then did this man, Jesus, become the one whose life and death has changed the world far beyond anyone before or after him? From a purely historical point of view, no other teaching or revelation of truth has had a more profound impact on culture, morality, politics, justice, philosophy, and most of all, freedom!

True Christianity always involves the freedom of individuals and nations. The apostle Paul wrote, "Now the Lord is the Spirit, and where the Spirit of the Lord is, there is freedom" (2 Corinthians 3:17). The mission of Jesus was to establish this freedom via the kingdom of God within the hearts and minds of all humanity. Love is the essence of this kingdom. The nature of this love is unselfish, without price, and meant to be shared openly in interpersonal relationships.

The Greek language of the New Testament uses the word *agape* to express this form of love. *Agape* is an unconditional love and carries within it the power to overcome the dilemmas of life.

Obviously and unfortunately, we people of the world don't exhibit this kind of *agape* love abundantly. Typically, it is *quid pro quo*—that is, "If you scratch my back, I'll scratch yours." In other words, the world exhibits mostly conditional love. Is this an indication that we have fallen short of Jesus' goal for us? Judging from the perspective of a humanity engulfed in the Existential Dilemma, the answer is unequivocally "Yes!"

But what if the message of Jesus' *agape* emanates from a source *outside* the time/space physical realm? This is a possibility that human beings in a material, time/space world find difficult to imagine or understand, but that does not make it impossible.

In the previous chapter, I introduced the enigmas of quantum physics, including Einstein's discoveries of relativity, the equivalencies of energy and matter, the wave/particle mystery, and the role consciousness plays in the formation of particles. **Theoretical physicists propose that invisible fields of energy, extending throughout the cosmos and penetrating material creation, are the source of power driving the creation of physical reality.** This is difficult for us to understand, but our lack of understanding does not make it untrue.[2]

Quantum physics theories like this are "radical" views of science when compared to Newton's clockwork universe. In presenting the message of Jesus' words and works, an equally radical view unfolds, emerging from sources beyond the time/space realm. The Existential Dilemma is a radical problem of the first order;

---

2. The proposed processes are called *baryogenesis*—which shows how protons and neutrons are created—and *leptogenesis*—how electrons are created.

radical problems demand radical answers! The foremost question is: "Does Jesus overcome the Existential Dilemma? How? Who then is this Jesus? Who does he claim to be, and what does he do to verify his claims?"

Enigmatic Jesus

Jesus was about 30 years old when he began his mission. Almost nothing is recorded about his developmental years with the exception of an encounter with teachers of the Jewish faith when he was 12 years old.

Along with his parents, relatives, and others, Jesus had traveled to Jerusalem to celebrate the Passover, an annual ceremony celebrating the Hebrew people's deliverance from Egypt, where they had lived in slavery. Upon the return journey to Nazareth, his parents discovered that Jesus was missing and returned to Jerusalem to find him. After three days, they found him in the temple, sitting among the teachers, listening to them and asking questions: "All who heard him were amazed at his understanding and the answers he gave" (Luke 2:47).

Jesus' parents were upset with him and did not understand his explanation, "How is it that you sought me? Did you not know that I must be in my father's house?" (Luke 2:49)

Apparently, Jesus understood his mission at a young age. What a vision he must have had—a vision that introduced a new view of reality! Any superficial assessment of his mission would quickly conclude: Mission: *Impossible*! In no way, manner, or form could a single human being accomplish such a lofty mission, let alone a boy 12 years of age. And yet, 20 years later, his final words upon the cross proclaimed, "It is finished!" (John 19:30) Mission: *Accomplished*!

In the next chapter, I have selected some examples of words spoken by Jesus that indicate his own perception of his purpose and his mission. These examples are among many words spoken directly by Jesus as portrayed in the four Gospels of the New Testament. For a more comprehensive picture of Jesus and his mission I suggest reading these four Gospels—Matthew, Mark, Luke, and John—in their entirety.

I am the Way the Truth & the Life

John 14:6

CHAPTER NINE

The Words of Jesus

"My kingdom is not of this world."
~JOHN 18:35A

*"You are from below; I am from above; you
are of this world. I am not of this world."*
~JOHN 8:23A

J esus clearly proclaimed that his kingdom is not *of* or *from* any construct of the physical world. His kingdom is present in the world but emanates from a source outside the time/space realm.

As strange as this appears to be, Jesus' description is very similar to descriptions of the discoveries of quantum physics. Recall the enigma of the wave/particle duality presented in Chapter Six. **All physical reality originates from unseen cosmic fields of energy.** These force fields are primary and foundational to all that physically exists. Human understanding and explanations of quantum realities are left hanging in a counterintuitive* state that defies complete analysis. Likewise, the kingdom of God originating "not from this world" eludes* human understanding and explanation. Some realities in life can be told but not explained.

Who Jesus Said He Was

"I and the Father are one."
~JOHN 10:30

While he was walking in the temple at Jerusalem, Jesus spoke these words to the Jewish religious leaders after a lengthy dialog with them. On many occasions, Jesus had referred to himself as "the Son of Man" and "the Son of God." He presented himself as having two natures, divine and human, integrated into one identity.

The Jewish religious leaders had grown increasingly threatened by the impact Jesus was having on the people, with his massive following and enigmatic message. Their tolerance had reached its limit! Now they were plotting to entrap him in a statement of blasphemy. On one occasion, the Jewish leaders surrounded him and demanded he tell them if he was the promised Messiah, the Christ. Knowing their treachery, he answered their request by revealing the true reason for their demand. He responded, "I have told you and you do not believe" (John 10:25).

Their problem with Jesus was of their own making—they did not believe him. He understood their failure to believe him but admonished* them to at least focus on the many good works shown to them "from the Father." There was no blasphemy. The words spoken by Jesus testified to his authenticity* and plainly revealed the truth: "The Father and I are one."

On another occasion, Jesus and his disciples were traveling from Judea to Galilee. When passing through Samaria, most people would take a rest stop in the city of Sychar. While they were there, the disciples went into the city to buy food. Jesus, wearied, stayed behind and rested at a well known as Jacob's Well.

According to John 4:1-26, Jesus chose to reveal himself to a Samaritan woman, an outsider, who had no motivation to resist him or his message. The woman came to draw water and Jesus asked her for a drink. An extensive conversation began that surprised the woman because Jews did not usually speak with Samaritans!

As they spoke, Jesus introduced the metaphor of "living water" that he could give the woman, and she would never thirst again. She responded, asking Jesus to give her this "living water" and end the drudgery of coming to the well. Recognizing her literal understanding of his words, Jesus clairvoyantly* proceeded to reveal to this stranger his awareness of her personal life. She then realized that she was speaking to a unique person: "Sir, I perceive that you are a prophet."

The Gospel of John concludes the conversation with her words: "I know the Messiah is coming; when he comes, he will show us all things," and Jesus' response, "I who speak to you am he" (John 4:26). With this simple statement, Jesus authenticated his mission and his purpose. Clearly, he laid claim to being the Messiah, or Christ.

Following are some other scriptures in which Jesus made statements about his purpose and identity:

John 12:46 *"I have come as light into the world, so that everyone who believes in me would not remain in darkness."* Jesus is generally recognized as a great teacher. Throughout his mission, he made generous use of analogies and parables to clarify* his teachings. In this verse, he portrays himself as the light that overcomes the darkness. All people are shrouded in this darkness and are unable to perceive the ultimate reality of their existence. We grope our way through life in blindness. Jesus reveals himself as the light that penetrates, dissipates,* and disperses* the darkness, enabling all who receive his message to live in the light. The only requirement is to believe in Jesus and the light he brings. I'm reminded of the prophetic declaration found in Isaiah 9:12, "The people who walked in darkness have seen a great light."

John 14:6 *"I am the way, and the truth, and the life. No one comes to the Father except through me."* Jesus spoke these words to Thomas, one of his 12 disciples. Thomas protested that he did not know where Jesus was going. So how could he know "the way"? This verse is part of a lengthy discourse* by Jesus pointing the way to the Father. The disciples were experiencing great difficulty trying to comprehend the spiritual nature of Jesus and his mission and revealing the all-too-common human need for concrete, physical explanations. Jesus emphasized the spiritual nature of his claim to be "the way, the truth, and the life." This is manifest in the very essence of his being, implied in his statement in John 10:30,

"The Father and I are one." To believe Jesus is to accept the Father into one's consciousness, since Jesus and the Father are one and the same. Jesus was introducing a new understanding into human experience that established the unification of the infinite and the finite. The nature of this new reality is spiritual, transcendent, and unbounded. Human consciousness receives it and lives it. No additional concepts are necessary since the "truth" is always singular, complete, and not paradoxical. With the authority of his personal identity, Jesus proclaimed that he alone is "the way, the truth, and the life." He alone perfectly bridges the estrangement of mankind from the Father, bridging our world and eternity.

John 3:14–15 *". . . and just as Moses lifted up the serpent in the wilderness, so must the Son of Man be lifted up, that whoever believes in him may have eternal life."* Throughout Jesus' mission of bringing the kingdom of God to the world, he repeatedly emphasized that his goal was to give eternal life to all who believe in him. What a preposterous* message—completely contrary to materialistic reason or finite common sense. We are left with two possible choices: either Jesus is a blithering* psychotic or he is proclaiming a revelatory* truth. To his disciples, he predicted his death by crucifixion and his resurrection from the dead. Overcoming death was an absolute essential in the fulfillment of Jesus' mission. Remember that death, as I have presented it, is the foundational dynamic and cause of the Existential Dilemma. **A true answer to this dilemma must arise from a realm outside of time/space.** Jesus' death by crucifixion and overpowering resurrection over death fulfilled this absolute demand for an answer.

Mark 10:45 *"For the Son of Man also came not to be served, but to serve and give his life a ransom for many."* Two brothers, James and John, disciples of Jesus, came to him with a special request that they would be seated on the right and left of Jesus when he came into his kingdom. Apparently assuming this meant that he would be the king of Israel (politically) and rule with authority, they wanted to be important in his cabinet. Jesus had a very different perspective and used the occasion to teach his disciples that greatness among them would be determined not by status but by servanthood. He included himself in this lesson, most significantly declaring that his destiny would be to give his life as a ransom* for many. How should the word "ransom" be understood? A ransom involves a payment made to redeem a person held in captivity. Jesus clearly understood that the human race was held in captivity by death, and the ransom to be paid was a sacrificial death by a worthy candidate. The Son of Man paid the price once and for all for all humanity. Jesus' death set the stage for his ultimate goal of overcoming death and freeing mankind from bondage.

Matthew 21:18–19 *"Behold, we are going up to Jerusalem; and the Son of Man will be delivered to the chief priests and scribes, and they will condemn him to death, and deliver him to the gentiles to be mocked and scourged and crucified on the third day."* Also, *in* **Mark 9:31**, Jesus was teaching his disciples, saying, *"The Son of Man will be delivered into the hands of men, and they will kill him; and when he is killed, after three days he will rise."* We are told that the disciples did not understand him when he spoke of his impending death and were afraid to ask him more. These comments, however, demonstrate the fact that Jesus knew exactly what would happen to him and why.

Matthew 28:18 *"And Jesus came and said to them, 'All authority in heaven and on earth has been given to me.'"* Imagine, if you can, a more powerful statement than this quote of Jesus, "All authority in heaven and earth has been given to me." Stated so simply, it nevertheless rises to a level of majesty. Jesus positions himself as the authority and power over heaven and earth, the whole universe, and all metaphysical reality. To accomplish his mission, such power was absolutely essential! Anything less would be a disclaimer,* and would place his mission under the control of the finite realm. To ransom the human race from the Existential Dilemma requires the revelation of an eternal reality. Jesus spoke these words to 11 of the disciples during one of his many physical appearances following his resurrection from the dead. The victory of his mission had been accomplished, and the disciples were being given the Great Commission:

Matthew 28:19–20 *"Go ye therefore and make disciples of all nations, baptizing them in the name of the Father and of the Son and of the Holy Spirit, teaching them to observe all things that I have commanded you; and lo, I am with you always, to the close of the age."* What a glorious promise to all of Jesus' followers, even to the present age!

Old and New Testament Scriptures contain many more references regarding Jesus' character and personhood besides the verses I have selected. Isaiah 53, for example, is highly prophetic concerning the sacrificial life and death of Jesus. The following verses convey the incarnational nature of Jesus' mission, bringing God and mankind into a personal and living relationship. These verses can be best understood in context. I advise reading the full accounts of when and why they were spoken.

John 18:36 *"My kingdom is not from this world."*

John 23a *"You are from below, I am from above; you are of this world, I am not of this world."*

John 9:5 *"As long as I am in the world, I am the light of the world."*

John 12:46 *"I have come as light into the world, so that everyone who believes in me should not remain in darkness."*

John 14:6 *"I am the way, the truth, and the life. No one comes to the Father, except through me."*

John 10:30 *"The Father and I are one."*

Luke 10:22 *"All things have been delivered to me by my Father; and no one knows who the Son is except the Father, or who the Father is except the Son and anyone to whom the Son chooses to reveal him."*

John 8:58 *"Before Abraham was, I am."*

John 12:32 *"And I, when I am lifted up from the earth I will draw all people to myself."*

John 8:28b *"I speak these things as the Father has instructed me."*

John 7:29 *"I know him because I am from him and he sent me."*

Mark 20:28 *"For the Son of Man also came not to be served but to serve and to give his life a ransom for many."*

John 2:19 *"Destroy this temple and in three days I will raise it up."*

John 4:26 *"Jesus said to her, 'I am he, the one who is speaking to you.'"*

Matthew 28:18 *"And Jesus came and said to them, 'All authority in heaven and on earth has been given to me.'"*

"Ask and it will be given to you." (Matthew 7:7)

CHAPTER TEN

The Works of Jesus

*"Miracles are not contrary to nature, but only
contrary to what we know about nature."*
~SAINT AUGUSTINE

*"The miracles of Jesus were the ordinary
works of the Father, wrought small and
swift that we might take them in."*
~GEORGE MACDONALD

Throughout the four New Testament Gospels, there are many, many accounts of Jesus performing what are called "miracles."* These include immediate healings of diseases such as blindness, deafness, leprosy, epilepsy, demon possessions, paralysis, and even raising the dead and subduing nature.

By human standards, these acts are contrary to human nature, human reason, and common sense. And yet, they were witnessed by hundreds and thousands of people over a period of three years in many parts of Israel. Great crowds followed Jesus wherever he went, and those whom he healed appeared to have ultimate faith in him.

How Jesus Revealed Himself as the Messiah

Jesus attributed his works to the Father, whose power and authority flowed through him: "For the works which the Father has granted me to accomplish these very works which I am doing, bear me witness that the Father has sent me" (John 5:36b).

What are we to make of these works of Jesus? The Bible does not provide us the mechanical details of the miracles. The best we can say initially is that some realities can be "told," but cannot be "explained."

Although quantum mechanics has clearly demonstrated that consciousness plays a prominent role in the collapse of the wave into a structured particle, and the cosmos is "entangled" at the microcosmic level, we should take caution not to suggest that Jesus' works can be defined by quantum science. Jesus' own explanation was clear: the Father was performing the miracles through him.

The purpose of Jesus' works was to demonstrate his power and authority over nature and all living things. This was absolutely required if the Existential Dilemma was to be overcome. As I have previously stressed, no answer to the dilemma is to be found within the physical domain of time/space. A new reality needed to be introduced, a reality not based on or in the physical domain, but capable of a full relationship with it. This new reality is "spiritual" and affirms consciousness as "eternal." This new reality transcends the Existential Dilemma and overcomes it by the so-called "miracles" that Jesus performed. **In other words, the infinite realm supersedes the finite realm.**

With this understanding, the meaningful purpose of Jesus' "miracles" is revealed. Jesus was fulfilling his mission of bringing the kingdom of God to humanity and ushering in a new concept of reality. He was establishing himself, his very being, as the transformative agent through whom the new understanding of reality would come to fruition.* Jesus' works were specifically enacted to accomplish this goal. His works clearly manifested his absolute authority and power over the physical domain, including the microcosm defined by quantum physics.

Identifying Jesus as the personification of the new reality, I have often thought of him as "Quantum Jesus." By his transcendent consciousness, he performed "miracles":

> *"Now when John heard in prison about the deeds of the Christ, he sent word by his disciples and said to him, 'Are you he who is to come or shall we look for another?'*
>
> *"And Jesus answered them, 'Go and tell John what you hear and see: the blind receive their sight and the lame walk, lepers are cleansed and the deaf hear, and the dead are raised up, and the poor have good news preached to them.'"*
> (Matthew 11:2–5)

Jesus affirms his response to John's inquiry that he is the Messiah, the Christ, and his works verify his identity.

The four Gospels report some of the many works performed by Jesus, but there were certainly more than are recorded for us. John tells us succinctly in the last verse of his gospel: "But there are also many other things that Jesus did; were every one to be written, I suppose that the world itself could not contain the books that would be written" (John 15:25).

The Healing of Jairus' Daughter

In the account of Mark 5: 35–43 and in Luke 8:41–42, followed by Luke 8:49–56, a man named Jairus, a ruler of the synagogue, came to Jesus. Falling at Jesus' feet, Jairus asked him to come to his house, where Jairus' only daughter, aged 12, was ill and dying. There was a crowd of people pressing Jesus, apparently delaying his immediate departure. A man from the ruler's household came and announced that the girl had died, so Jairus should not trouble Jesus any longer.

Jesus answered, "Do not fear, only believe, and she will be well." He arrived at the house to find the family and others weeping and wailing. They laughed at him when he said, "She is sleeping," because they knew she was dead.

Jesus went into the room where the body lay and said, "Child, arise." Luke then states that her spirit returned! There is no explanation capable of describing what was really happening in this account. Again, Jesus was demonstrating his power and transcendence over life and death. The requirement of Jairus was to "only believe," or have faith that Jesus could return life to his daughter.

Believing is an intentional act of the conscious mind. Christ is inviting us to believe, thus engaging our consciousness with his.

The Woman in the Crowd

Sandwiched within both Mark's and Luke's gospel accounts of the raising of Jairus' daughter is the report of a woman in a crowd who'd had a chronic flow of blood for 12 years. She came up behind Jesus and touched the fringe of his garment and immediately sensed that she was healed. Jesus asked who had touched him. No one responded; Peter offered the fact that many in the crowd had touched him. But Jesus persisted, "for I perceive that power has gone forth from me."

The woman wanted to be incognito but realized she couldn't hide. She admitted why she had touched him, telling the people present how she had been healed. Jesus replied to her, "Your faith has made you well. Go in peace." In this event (recorded for us in Luke 8:43–48), Jesus did nothing voluntarily and yet was conscious of power leaving him. What was this power? Any definition is beyond human capability. And yet, this woman had access to it by faith. This, I believe, is the important point. **Faith can grasp power through an intentional conscious act.**

The Raising of Lazarus

In John 11:25-26, Jesus stated, "I am the resurrection and the life. Those who believe in me, even though they die, will live, and everyone who lives and believes in me will never die. Do you believe this?" Jesus spoke these words to Martha, whose brother Lazarus had died four days earlier. Jesus was a close friend to Martha, Mary, and Lazarus, and had been informed of Lazarus' illness.

Knowing that Lazarus had already died, Jesus delayed his departure two days.

When he arrived at Bethany, Lazarus had been entombed four days. Both sisters were critical of Jesus for delaying his arrival and believed Lazarus would have been alive had Jesus not tarried. Apparently, they had no faith that Jesus could raise him from the dead.

There was a sizeable group of people present who had come to console the sisters, and Jesus prayed to the Father that they would believe that Jesus was sent by the Father. He then cried with a loud voice, "Lazarus come out." The dead man came out, his hands and feet bound with bandages, and his face wrapped with a cloth. Jesus said to them, "Unbind him, and let him go." This miracle was a profound act, and the Jewish leaders realized they could no longer tolerate Jesus and his works. This miracle was the straw that "broke the camel's back."

The Centurion's Servant

We will assume that the centurion was a Roman who was in charge of 100 occupational troops. His servant was paralyzed, at home, and in terrible distress.

The centurion came to Jesus and asked for Jesus' help. Jesus answered him, "I will come and heal him." The centurion responded that he was unworthy to have Jesus come under his roof, but if Jesus would just say the word, his servant would be healed. Jesus marveled at the centurion's response, saying, " 'Truly, I say to you, not even in Israel have I found such faith. Go; be it done to you as you have believed.' The servant was healed at that very moment" (Matthew 8:5-13).

The significant point to be made in this miracle is that the healing took place immediately at a distance and was based on a person's faith. Again, this event can be told, but not explained.

The Canaanite Woman

Matthew 15:21-28 finds Jesus and his disciples in the area of Tyre and Sidon. These were coastal cities about twenty miles apart. A Gentile* woman confronted Jesus respectfully, but insistently. She addressed him: "Have mercy on me. O Lord, Son of David; my daughter is severely possessed by a demon." But he did not answer her a word.

The disciples begged Jesus to send her away because she was pestering them. Finally, Jesus answered her, explaining that he was sent only to the lost people of Israel. She knelt before him and pleaded. "Lord, help me."

He responded, "It is not fair to take the children's bread and throw it to the dogs."

Was she offended by Jesus' apparent rudeness? Apparently not, because she replied, "Yes, Lord, yet even the dogs eat the crumbs that fall from their master's table."

Then Jesus answered her, "O woman, great is your faith! Be it done to you as you desire." Her daughter was healed instantly!

Several of Jesus' many miracles involved people who were not Jewish, demonstrating the fact that he is the Savior of all mankind, not just the people of Israel.

The Resurrection of Jesus

In Matthew 21:18-19, Jesus told his 12 disciples, "Behold, we are going up to Jerusalem; and the Son of Man will be delivered to the chief priests and scribes, and they will condemn him to death, and deliver him to the gentiles to be mocked and scourged and crucified, and he will be raised on the third day." And, in Mark 9:30-31, we read, "They went on from there and passed through Galilee. And he would not have anyone know it for he was teaching his disciples saying to them, 'The Son of Man will be delivered into the hands of men, and they will kill him; and when he is killed after three days he will rise!'" Jesus spoke to his disciples very clearly and directly, but they did not understand. Jesus' triumphant entry into a hotbed of political turmoil, the city of Jerusalem, ended with his ignominious death by crucifixion and the triumph of his resurrection, just as he had foretold them.

It was absolutely essential that Jesus overcame death in order for his mission to be fulfilled. His overcoming of death was at the same time the overcoming of the Existential Dilemma for those who believe in him and in his message of peace and love.

"Behold, I stand at the door and knock." (*Revelation 3:20*)

CHAPTER ELEVEN

The Triumph of Faith

By Erik Ogard

"Faith is like an empty, open hand
stretched out towards God, with nothing
to offer and everything to receive."
~JOHN CALVIN

The previous chapter concludes my father's writing. At the time of his passing, Don had drafted every chapter of this book with the exception of this one, the final chapter, which, in our family, we refer to as "the faith chapter." He left a rough—but incomplete—draft and notes on the importance of personal faith in Jesus as it relates to solving the Existential Dilemma, but he ran out of time before he could finish it. We promised him we would finish this chapter and publish his book.

Don's view was that personal faith in Jesus—made possible by our consciousness and our conscious intention—provides the only solution to humanity's existential crisis. Faith in Jesus, thus, is the final piece as it relates to solving the

Existential Dilemma puzzle. While this book is not an apologetics* piece for Christianity per se,* it is based on my father's view that Jesus is *the only solution* to the Existential Dilemma. The final step of faith, then, is each of ours to freely make. In the pages that follow, we will consider personal faith in Christ as it relates to our personal Existential Dilemma. I believe unequivocally that Jesus Christ is who he claimed to be: that he is God, incarnate. The purpose in stipulating* faith, rather than trying to convince the reader, is to introduce the broader architecture of the Existential Dilemma and the essential role faith plays in solving it.

There are countless Christian apologetics works by biblical scholars aimed at convincing people through facts and reason that this is true. If the reader finds they would like additional perspective, I recommend the timeless book *Mere Christianity* by C. S. Lewis. More broadly, if you need convincing, I encourage you to seek out this and other apologetic works and read them. There is no more important question to be answered in your life!

For now, I will explore the relationship between personal faith in Christ and how that faith overcomes the Existential Dilemma.

> *"To one who has faith, no explanation is necessary.*
> *To one without faith, no explanation is possible."*
> ~Thomas Aquinas
>
> *"Faith sees the invisible, believes the unbelievable, and receives the*
> *impossible."*
> ~Corrie Ten Boom

It may be the case that the mere understanding of how faith in Christ works to solve the biggest problems human beings face could be enough to convince you, or to support your decision if you have already believed.

An Overview: The Architecture of the Dilemma and the Solution

Don has made the case that the source of human consciousness is a total mystery to mankind; both from the objective perspective of science and the subjective perspective of reason. We know nothing of its source or basic nature. We can describe how consciousness operates and much of what you've read in this book comes from this type of inquiry. We've even speculated that the source of consciousness might be external to the brain itself—a fundamental force within the universe on par with gravity.

Whatever the ultimate source, the Existential Dilemma resides in human consciousness. Anxiety, a psychological response to the Existential Dilemma, also resides in the conscious experience. Anxiety takes up residency* within the conscious experience right alongside transcendent awareness; so, consciousness is simultaneously a great strength and a great weakness.

This fundamental reality—the reality of consciousness, the Existential Dilemma, and anxiety—is intractable without some external, interrupting force. We have described how a man-made finite solution from within this world simply cannot solve a problem of transcendent origin. Don described such a solution as being akin* to someone lifting themselves by their own bootstraps: it is not possible. That is why he proposed this "interrupting force" to be the life, death, and resurrection of Jesus Christ. It seemed logical to him that this interrupting force would be from an eternal reality outside of time and space: a transcendent (infinite) problem requires a transcendent (infinite) solution. This is the setup into which personal faith enters: it is the final step in resolving the Existential Dilemma.

The Nature of the Existential Dilemma

We humans occupy a unique place in the cosmos, primarily because of our transcendent consciousness. This condition places us in a superior position over the purely material realm and establishes freedom of being (will, choice, and sovereignty). However, our bodies exist purely within the material realm and occupy the finite time/space reality. This creates a mysterious union of the infinite (our transcendent consciousness) and finite (our temporal bodies) within each person and circumscribes* both strength and weakness in the human psyche. Especially, it creates the basis of anxiety, because we know with certainty that our physical lives will come to a permanent end.

Our consciousness rightly rejects this state of affairs and is in mortal combat with every threat to our existence. In the end, in this drama of earthly existence, we die: "Of dust are we made; to dust we shall return" (Genesis 3:19). Are we only physical beings or are we both physical and metaphysical beings? Does our consciousness continue after our physical lives end?

In vain, humanity has searched for an earthly resolution to this dilemma. We have developed governments, social programs, educational programs, rehabilitation programs, and the like, all aimed either directly or indirectly at the Existential Dilemma and the distress it creates in people. In fact, it is finitude that separates humans from the infinite, causing the dilemma.

Humans, in expressing their free will and sovereignty, have chosen to separate the natural union of the infinite and the finite—and place themselves as rulers of the finite realm. In hubris,* humans have ignorantly claimed isolated ownership over the physical world, thus breaking the union of the infinite and the finite and creating a gap that cannot be filled. In religious terms, this is known as the fall of humanity, which is the cause of the separation of God (infinite) and man (finite).

It seems obvious that the finite realm has no ability or power to recapture the infinite (i.e., earth cannot capture heaven). Thus, if a reunion of the two realms is going to be accomplished, it must proceed from the infinite! The truth is all too apparent—there is no resolution to be found in the finite world because the dilemma is rooted within the human transcendent consciousness. Therefore, it follows that any resolution of this dilemma must be fundamentally transcendent.

The Nature of Faith

It should not come as a surprise that the word "faith" should enter into the discussion, since it has come up several times in this book. What may come as a surprise to some, however, is the concept of faith viewed as a *force* that has the capacity to overcome the juggernaut* of the dilemma. It all depends on how one understands the reality of faith.

Edward O. Wilson, the preeminent biologist and naturalist, states in his 2015 book, *The Meaning of Human Existence* (page 154): "Faith is the one thing that makes otherwise good people do bad things." Atheists, such as Richard Dawkins, view faith as an illusion or a delusion. They define faith as "blind faith"—a belief in something or someone without physical evidence. This is, of course, the interpretation of faith by a materialist scientist. It is also the common view of much of the general public. Proof and evidence must be confirmed by empirical* facts. This is not the understanding of faith we present here.

There are two kinds of faith. The first is not the kind of faith Jesus spoke about but is the kind of faith that is typically expressed by human beings relative to material existence. We have faith in the physical world based upon familiarity. The earth will continue spinning. The sun will come up. Rain will fall, and soil will continue to provide the food we need for our sustenance.

We also have faith in institutions that we trust—governments, corporations, religions, and individual human beings whom we have experienced to be trustworthy.

The other kind of faith—the kind that Jesus spoke of—comes not from the finite world, but from eternity. According to theologian Paul Tillich, "Faith is an act of a finite being who is grasped by, and has turned to, the infinite." The transcendent consciousness, the recipient "being grasped," experiences faith as being certain.

Don spent a lot of time thinking about the human experience as being bifurcated between subjective reality and objective reality. This bifurcation is helpful in thinking about the faith experiences we have been discussing so far in this chapter. Note that both sides of the divide are "real" expressions of existence, but expressed very differently. As can be seen in the table below, the faith to which Jesus is inviting us resides in the mind, which is to say it is a subjective rather than an objective experience. The subjective nature of faith can make it difficult for some people who are oriented toward the objective, material world to understand. Please note, importantly, that the things discussed in this book—consciousness, anxiety, the Existential Dilemma, and faith—all reside in the subjective column of human reality.

Subjective	Objective
Idealism	Materialism
Mind	Body
Essence	Existence
Quality	Quantity
Color	Wave length
Art	Science
Internal World	Physical World
Emotions	Facts

According to new findings of quantum physics, the external, physical world is a phantasm, the internal world of the conscious mind is the real world. It is necessary, therefore, to demonstrate how Christian faith has accomplished the overcoming of this bifurcation between subjective and objective expressions of reality, and of the Existential Dilemma, with its power of death and resulting anxiety. It must be understood that anything produced by human reason, creativity, or effort is enclosed within a finite cocoon. The finite cannot incorporate the infinite. It is the infinite that must incorporate the finite.

Basically, any experience of faith involves two components. One component is the origin of whatever is deemed to be acceptable, trustworthy, or believed. The other component is the reception of this information and the decision whether or not to accept it as presented by the originator.

This accepting and approving response is called "faith," and is generic* in human relations. For example, this includes trust in the roles of governments and the operations of corporations. Promises made to the citizens, their customers, and shareholders are accepted in faith. In fact, this is true of all institutions and organizations offering goods and services to a trusting public.

All of science lives within this framework of faith, in spite of claims to the contrary. Consider what has happened to the science of physics since Sir Isaac Newton discovered what was considered to be a universe of certainty and predictability. Along came Einstein, Bohr, Heisenberg, and many others, astounding the world with theories of uncertainty, the relativity of time/space, and unpredictability. We now live in a world of probabilities. Science, therefore, lives by faith, as does all of humanity. We live in a reality of an unknown and unpredictable future. As the existentialists among us proclaim, "There is no exit."

Do Christian believers live in a faith that is fundamentally different from this? The answer is both "no" and "yes." The "no" acknowledges the common components of the faith transaction—the original sender of the information and the receiver of the information. Also, there is acknowledgement of the receivers' acceptance, response, trust, and confidence in the sender's offering.

The "yes," however, acknowledges a vast difference between what can be called "secular" faith and "Christian" faith. The difference rests with the nature of the content of what is being sent, the avenue taken by the information, and the capacity of the receiver to accept the information.

Our Christian faith is dependent on the information, activity, and promises of a God who revealed his messages through the ancient prophets and finally through the life, death, and resurrection of Jesus, the Messiah. The difference is that information is communicated from the realm of the eternal and does not originate from within the time/space framework. As we have previously noted, Jesus proclaimed that his kingdom was not of this world. His message carries the power to overcome the infinite divide separating the temporal from the eternal. This was demonstrated by his superiority and control over physical reality and most profoundly by his power over death. All of this emanates from the transcendent realm of the eternal.

Is it possible for a human being to be grafted* and integrated into this realm? This is the crucial* question. Also crucial is the transcendent nature of consciousness. Being transcendent, consciousness is capable of resonating with and experiencing the presence of that which is greater than its own thinking capacity. In other words, human consciousness is, within itself, limited in its capacity to fully comprehend the eternal, let alone the capacity to encompass it. Consciousness does recognize the mystery beyond itself but has no ability to venture beyond the confines of its limitations.

Therefore, if there is to be any relationship with the eternal, the eternal must grasp, encompass, and infiltrate the human's consciousness. This is exactly the proclamation* of the gospel of Jesus, the Christ, the bedrock of Christian faith. It's a gift of unfathomable reality.

Faith Is a Personal Choice for Every Individual

Faith is totally and completely a gift of the eternal Creator of the cosmos. To accept this gift, a person must be open to receiving its message. Our human nature can voice a yes or a no to its reception. Its acceptance creates faith within the being of consciousness. **This faith, therefore, is transcendent and is composed of the power to nullify* and overcome the power of anxiety.** This power comes to the accepting person not from the material or philosophical realm of the polarized world, but through a created relationship with and by a personal loving God. This eternal faith is manifest in the being and spiritual presence of Jesus, the Christ, who overcame and nullified the power of death. This alone negates the dilemma of human existence.

The message of the freeing power of faith in Jesus Christ carries within it the certainty of its truth. Its origin emanates not from division or polarization but from the singular being of the indwelling and eternal God. **In other words, what human beings are totally unable to accomplish has become a new reality as a completed gift. To accept the gift brings peace; to reject it continues life in the Existential Dilemma.**

The apostle John, author of the Book of Revelation in the New Testament, described the nature of the Christian faith very succinctly: "Behold, I stand at the door and knock; if anyone hears My voice and opens the door, I will come in to him, and will dine with him, and he with me" (Revelation 3:30). This is a metaphor of the process of becoming a believer, or a "person of faith." It describes a person who is present within the confines of his home, perceives a knocking on the door, and hears someone speaking. He or she must make decision to respond and open the door or to ignore the one knocking. The person within the house has the freedom to do either.

If, and this is a big if, he or she decides to open the door and allow the person outside to enter, there is a promise of mutual friendship, fellowship, and life-sustaining nurture. This is not forceful entry (nor has any previous invitation been extended by the homeowner). The verse doesn't present any conclusion but makes it clear that the motive and dynamics of the visit are completely up to the one knocking; the homeowner is the recipient and merely need open and receive the good intentions of the visitor. Such is the substance of Christian faith, which follows as one accepts the promise of eternal life.

Following is a Bible study Don prepared and presented to his church council on the verse above. It is my hope you find this helpful as you consider your response to the faith invitation. It is your choice and your choice alone as a sovereign entity.

The Metaphor of the Door

"Listen! [Behold], I am standing at the
door knocking; If you hear my voice
and open the door I will come into you
and eat with you, and you with me."
~REVELATION 3:20, NRSV

1. **"Listen!"** Pay attention to this (some translations say "Behold!"), this is *very* important!
2. **"I"** (Jesus is speaking.) What I am about to say is very personal. It comes to you from the heart of my being. This is what my mission is, to seek and save the lost.
3. **". . . am standing . . ."** I have taken a position in reference to you. I'm not budging, I'm standing pat.
4. **". . . at the door . . ."** There is a separation between us and you cannot see me. But I am very close by.
5. **". . . knocking . . ."** I am politely trying to get your attention. I am not going to forcefully invade your space.
6. **". . . if . . ."** I recognize your freedom. You have a decision to make. The choice is up to you to respond to the knocking or ignore the knocking.
7. **". . . you . . ."** This involves you personally. It's you I'm interested in.

8. **". . . hear my voice . . ."** Listen! I have a message for you—I'm speaking, but you may not get what I'm saying from behind the closed door. Are you curious? Are you motivated to respond?

9. **". . . and . . ."** An additional important step is involved. At this point you can choose not to answer the door.

10. **". . . open the door . . ."** The knock and voice could be a stranger—there is a degree of risk and annoyance. You have the ability to not open the door, but you can also open the door and see "what gives."

11. **"I will come in to you."** No invitation has been extended to this stranger. His presence must be compelling and it is clear he wants to enter. It's almost like a promise: "I will come in."

12. **". . . and eat with you, and you with me."** If I am welcomed in, you will experience a very personal, nurturing relationship. It will be a friendship on an equal basis. I have a gift of faith to offer you that overcomes the world of anxiety, misery, doubt, and death.

Chapters 2 and 3 of the New Testament's book of Revelation are directed to seven churches that were established in the first century AD. Each church was given recognition for its strength and loyalty but strongly criticized for its failings.

Laodicea was the seventh church to be examined. It was neither hot nor cold, and was not recognizing that it was "pitiable, wretched, poor, blind, and naked." Verse 3:19 says, "Those whom I love, I reprove and chasten; so be zealous and repent."

Revelation 3:20 portrays the foundation on which the church must stand. **It must be based on a personal relationship with Jesus by each individual believer**.

Christian faith is transmitted to the receiving person's consciousness. This consciousness has defied definition because of its total subjectivity. This point is important: Christian faith originates and is conceived within the eternal realm. It follows, therefore, that this faith defies definition also. There is nothing objective about it. Human consciousness receives, resonates, and experiences the unlimited power of its presence within the self or being.

This creates a new reality for the person who accepts the offer. It is a reality of love and redemption given to a humanity lost in the clutches of the Existential Dilemma. It promises life eternal here and now. This Christian faith overcomes the power of death and its accompanying anxiety. This is the completed, triumphant, and victorious gift to the world. It is completely transcendent.

Does this mean that evil and its power have been banished from the earth? By no means! Death and destruction remain and continue. But the peace that surpasses all understanding rests within the souls, hearts, and minds of those who accept the message of eternal rescue.

What has changed is that transcendent consciousness no longer exists in isolation and vulnerability in a world of death and destruction but is affirmed in its transcendence by the eternal power of its Creator. This is the new reality that is present in the world. It promises love, abiding presence, and life eternal to anyone who accepts the gift of faith.

As I have emphasized earlier, this message carries within it the certainty of its truth, emanating from the singular being of the indwelling and eternal God. Certainty is a reality within Christian faith because what is eternal cannot contain anything other than what it is—infinite constancy without change or alteration. It is what is. Uncertainty is not a possibility except in the temporal realm. Because of this truth, Christian faith and its eternal nature present to humanity a new reality that overcomes the power of the Existential Dilemma.

Don's belief was that the Existential Dilemma was overcome two thousand years ago by the life, death, and resurrection of Jesus Christ. Importantly, this overcoming came from outside of the physical world.

For all of those who do not believe in eternal life, the world in which we live is the only acknowledged reality. But, for those who believe in Jesus, we live in eternity *now*. This does not mean our earthly lives are totally free from sin or anxiety, but it does mean that Christians on earth live in hope of a heavenly eternity completely free from evil, sin, tragedy, and the Existential Dilemma. This triumphant faith provides the only genuine relief from the intrinsic anxiety that plagues humanity. We Christians are in the world, but not of it. In contrast, in the physical world of entropy, mankind has found no solution to the great dilemma.

As Don believed and often said, "It should not surprise us that the Creator and Sustainer of the universe is and always will be intellectually ahead of mankind. It takes the infinite to overcome the finite world in which we live!"

"This do in remembrance of me." (Luke 22:19)

Glossary

Words and Phrases Used by the Author
Indicated by * throughout this Book

Absolute (philosophy): ultimate or most supreme; usually conceived of as either encompassing the sum of all being, actual and potential or otherwise transcending the concept of "being" altogether; free from imperfections; perfect with no exceptions or qualifications

AD: *Anno Domini*, "In the Year of Our Lord," synonymous with CE, or "Common Era"

Addictive (psychology): habit-forming substances and behaviors that have harmful psychological and social effects, typically causing well-defined symptoms such as anxiety, irritability, tremors, nausea, etc.

Ad Infinitum: without end or limit; to infinity; having no end

Admonish: to urge someone to do something; to remind someone of an obligation or responsibility; to counsel against something

Affirm: to assert to be true; to declare support for or belief in; to state positively and firmly

Akin: having some of the same qualities or character; sharing common origins

Allegory: a representation of an abstract or spiritual meaning through concrete or material forms; figurative treatment of one subject under the guise of another

Ambiguity: something that can be understood in more than one way; doubtfulness or uncertainty as regards the interpretation of something

Analogy: a comparison between two things that are different, but have some similar features; often used to explain a principle, not just to make a comparison, but to also provide an explanation of a concept; often expressed as "something is like something else"

Anomaly: deviation from the normal or common rule in type, arrangement, or form

Antithesis: direct contrast; opposition; direct or exact opposite; absolute opposite

Anxiety: the vague state of unspecified uncertainty common to all human beings

Apologetics: argumentative discourse in defense of the Christian faith by delving into philosophical theology; the branch of theology that is concerned with defending the truth of Christian doctrine

Arbiter: someone who makes a judgment, solves an argument, or decides what will be done; someone who is considered to be authoritative or worthy of respect

Architecture: both the process and design of a particular concept or idea; most commonly used in reference to buildings

Ascetics: persons who practice strict self-denial and lead an austere life as a measure of personal, and especially spiritual, discipline

Astrophysical: referring to astronomical phenomena such as the physical properties, behaviors, and dynamic processes of celestial objects

Atheistic Materialist: a person who assumes that the physical universe and its properties are all that exist and that nothing exists outside the material world; according to this view a transcendent God cannot exist

Atom: the irreducible smallest particle of an element that can exist alone or in combination as a constituent of a specified system; considered to be a source of vast potential constructive or destructive energy

Atonement: reparation made for an injury or wrong; reconciliation with God by repentance and confession of one's sins; reconciliation of God and humans brought about by the redemptive life and death of Jesus

Authenticity: quality of being trustworthy, genuine; entitled to acceptance as authoritative; true and correct

Axes: plural form of axis; often used to describe lines that cross vertically at right angles to each other to create sections on a graph

Axis: an invisible line going through the center of an object around which objects rotate or may be conceived to rotate; or a straight line around which things are evenly arranged, as in a chart or graph

BC: "Before Christ," also commonly BCE or "Before the Common Era," which begins with Year 1 in the Gregorian calendar

Behaviorism: a school of psychology that confines itself to the study of observable and quantifiable aspects of behavior and excludes subjective phenomena, such as emotions or motives

Bifurcation: the act of dividing one thing or one concept into two parts or branches

Blithering: Talking incoherently; jabbering nonsense; making no sense whatsoever

Boson: a subatomic particle that carries any of the four fundamental actions of nature; detected through a discrete quantum field that is emitted and can be measured in elementary particles (a theoretical unit of measurement)

Broken Symmetry (physics): A phenomenon in which infinitesimally small fluctuations acting on a system crossing a critical point decide the system's fate by determining which branch of a bifurcation is taken

Cartesianism: of or relating to the philosophy of René Descartes; a form of rationalism because it holds that scientific knowledge can be derived from *a priori* innate ideas through deductive reasoning

Caste System: a class structure that is determined by birth; divides people on the basis of inherited social status (India has been a well-known example of a caste system)

CE: the Common or Current Era, which begins with Year 1 on the Gregorian calendar; synonymous with AD (*Anno Domini*, "The Year of Our Lord," referring to Christ)

Chimera: a fire-breathing she-monster in Greek mythology, having a lion's head, a goat's body, and a serpent's tail

Circumscribe: to construct or be constructed around; to draw a line around; to define or mark off carefully; to constrict/eliminate other choices

Clairvoyant: having great, unexplainable insight not perceived by the senses; a person appearing to know about things or events that cannot be perceived by the senses

Clarify: make an idea, statement, etc. clear and understandable; make something free from ambiguity or confusion

Coalesce: to come or grow together in a single mass; to come together as a recognizable whole or entity; to come together for a single purpose; the process by which two particles merge during contact to form a single particle (think of two drops of water merging to form one drop)

Cogency: power of compelling conviction; credibility; being reasonable and persuasive

Cognitive Therapy: a system of psychotherapy involving the analysis of individual episodes of social interaction for insights that will aid communication

Communist: person who believes in or promotes the replacement of private ownership and profit-based economies with a classless economic system under which the means of production are communally owned and private ownership of property is either prohibited or severely restricted by the government

Complementary: forming or serving as a complement; completing; offsetting mutual deficiencies or enhancing mutual strengths

Consciousness: considered to be difficult to define because of its subjective nature; self-awareness; awareness of external stimuli and internal stimuli, including feelings of hunger, thirst, etc., and being aware of our thoughts and emotions as well as external surroundings and events

Construct (noun): a theory or complicated idea created by making several simpler ideas fit together; ideas formed, shaped, and developed in the human mind

Continuum: continuous series of elements or items that vary by such tiny differences, they do not seem to differ from each other (example: continuous temperatures from freezing to boiling)

Conundrum: a paradoxical, insolvable, or difficult problem; a dilemma

Copenhagen Interpretation: the act of observation collapses the wave function in a wave-particle exchange; a theory in quantum physics

Cosmos/Cosmological: the physical universe considered as a totality of phenomena in time and space

Counterintuitive: contrary to what common sense would indicate or suggest; not easily understood in an instinctive, unconscious way

Crucial: extremely significant or important; vital to the resolution of a crisis or the determination of an outcome

Dark Energy: inferred by our observation that the universe is expanding at an accelerated rate (We don't know what is driving the accelerated expansion; to be expanding at an increasingly accelerated rate it must have energy, so we are calling it dark energy)

Dark Matter: matter that doesn't interact with the electromagnetic force and doesn't absorb, reflect, or emit light (humans are only able to infer its existence from its apparent gravitational effect on visible matter)

Datum: a fact or proposition used to draw a conclusion or make a decision

Demise: the end of existence or activity; death

Deterministic: causally determined and not subject to random chance; a philosophy that everything that happens must happen as the inevitable consequence of antecedent states of affairs (according to this view there is no free will)

Deterrent: serving to discourage, inhibit or prevent something from happening

Dialectic: arriving at the truth by the exchange of logical arguments; arriving at truth by thesis, developing a contrary antithesis, and resolving them into a coherent synthesis

Dichotomous: divided or dividing into two parts

Dichotomy: a division into two contrasting things or forms; branching characterized by successive forking into two approximately equal divisions; the drawing of a clear division into two parts or kinds, etc.

Differentiate: to make different by mediation or alteration; to perceive or show the difference between things

Diffraction/Diffraction Pattern: the bending of waves, especially sound and light waves around obstacles in their path; the distinctive pattern of light and dark fringes, rings, etc. that are formed by diffraction

Disclaimer: denial of responsibility for something; a disowning; renunciation

Discourse: lengthy treatment of a subject, either written or spoken about a particular, usually serious, subject

Disperse: scatter in different directions; distribute widely; to cause to attenuate or disappear; to cause to spread, as in news

Dissipate: cause to scatter, render irreversibly gone

Domain: a sphere of activity, influence, or knowledge; a field of action, thought, influence; a territory over which control is exercised

Dormancy: not active or growing, but able to become active later

Dualistic/duality: the quality or state of having two different parts, or two opposite parts; the quality or character of being twofold; dichotomy; two subcases of opposite parts (example: wave/particle)

Dualism/Dualistic (philosophy): 1. the view that the world consists of or is explicable as two fundamental entities such as mind and matter; 2. the concept that the mind is more than just the brain; that the mind has a nonmaterial, spiritual dimension that includes consciousness and possibly an eternal attribute

Dualistic (physics): the mathematical equivalence of two seemingly different descriptions of a physical system

Dysfunction: abnormal or impaired functioning; failure to achieve or sustain a behavioral norm, as in a social relationship; failure to function in an expected or complete manner

Electrodynamics: the study of moving electrical charges and their interaction with the electric and magnetic fields; the phenomena associated with these interactions

Electromagnetic Force (one of the four forces of physics): the force that occurs between electrically charged particles; exhibits magnetic forces such as magnetic fields, electric fields, and lights

Electron: an elementary particle that is a fundamental constituent of matter; exists independently or as the component outside the nucleus of an atom; subatomic particle whose electric charge is negative one elementary charge

Elude: to be too difficult to understand or remember; to escape from memory or understanding of something; to be unattained

Emanate: issue from something, flow out of something, proceed outward from something

Embedded: caused to be an integral part of a surrounding whole; fixed or strongly enclosed in a surrounding mass

Empirical: verifiable or provable by observation or experiment; guided by practical experience and not theory

Empiricist: one holding the view that experience, especially that of the senses, is the only source of knowledge; the employment of empirical methods in science; all matters of fact come from experience and need experience for validation

Encapsulated: surrounded entirely by something else; enclosed within

Enigma: a puzzling, ambiguous, or inexplicable statement, occurrence, or situation

Enlightenment: the pinnacle of human development and potential; being advanced and having gained necessary knowledge, especially spiritual knowledge

(The) Enlightenment (1700–1800): a movement in the 18th century that stressed the belief that science and logic give people more knowledge and understanding than tradition and religion

Enmeshed: tangled or twisted together; caught as if in a mesh

Entangled: deeply involved, especially with something complicated or confusing; wrapped or twisted together

Entanglement (physics): a physical phenomenon that occurs when a group of particles are generated, interact, or share spatial proximity in a way such that the quantum state of each particle in the group cannot be described independently of the state of the others, even when the particles are separated by a large distance; entangled particles remain connected so that actions performed on one affect the other, even when separated by long distances

Entities: things that exist apart from other things, having their own independent existence

Entropy (physics): a measure of unavailable energy in a closed system, associated with a disorder or uncertainty in a system

Essence: The inherent, unchanging nature of a thing or a class of things; the indispensable quality or qualities that serve to identify something; the real, ultimate nature of a thing as opposed to its existence

Estrangement: state of being alienated or separated in feeling; broken, disrupted relationship; division, disunity, disassociation

Eternal: infinite; without beginning or ending

Ethereal: spiritual or otherworldly; regions beyond the earth

Evolutionists: people who believe in the theory of biological evolution, especially the theory formulated by Charles Darwin

Exigencies: difficulties of a situation that cause urgent demands; pressing or urgent situations

Existential: belonging to existence; the fact or state of physical being in a material world

Existentialism (philosophy): a form of philosophical inquiry that explores the problem of human existence and centers on the experience of thinking, feeling, and acting in the face of an apparently meaningless world

Existential Dilemma: the sense of anxiety inherent within every human being; the human problem of being essentially spiritual beings in physical bodies in a material, physical world

Expanded (psychology): increased in scope or quality

Exponentially: many times, as raising a quantity to a power

Fermion (physics): elementary or composite particle such as an electron, quark, or proton, whose spin is an integer multiple of 12

Field (physics): a physical quantity assigned to every point in space (or more generally time/space); a field extends over a large region of space so that it influences everything (for example— objects fall to the ground on earth because the objects are affected by the force of the earth's gravitational field)

Finite/Finitude: having boundaries, limits, end/the state of having boundaries, limits, end

First Cause: source or cause of something else; God as the uncaused creator of all beings apart from himself; self-created source of all being; first associated with Thomas Aquinas (1225–1274 AD), the idea that everything that exists has a causal chain leading ultimately to God

Forces (physics): external agents that produce motion or change

Foundational: forming the base from which everything else develops

Fruition: the attainment or realization of something desired, worked out, or accomplished

Fusion: two or more things joined into one thing or combined into one thing

Fusion (physics): a dominant source of energy for stars in the universe and potential energy source on earth; combining lighter atomic nuclei to form a heavier nucleus

Gamma Rays: rays that rise from the radioactive decay of atomic nuclei; shortest wavelength of all electromagnetic waves; highest energy form of light

Geiger Counter: a device used to measure particles in ionized gasses; widely used in applications like radiological protection, experimental physics, and the nuclear industry

Generic: general; relating to or descriptive of an entire group or class; lacking specificity

Genome: complete genetic information of an organism; can be either DNA or RNA; found in the middle of a cell; containing all chromosomes that encode the genetic material of the cell

Gentile: a person who is not Jewish; a heathen or pagan

Gluons: massless force-mediating particles that exist in every atomic nucleus, holding it together, and bind subatomic particles known as quarks within the protons and neutrons of stable matter as well as within heavier, short-lived particles created by high energies

God Particle: the particle that gives mass to matter—also known as the Higgs boson

Grafted: caused to unite; to be implanted into something else

Gravitational Force (one of the four forces of physics): the weakest of the four forces; long range but relatively weak force of attraction that acts between all particles that have mass; the force of attraction between all the masses in the universe

Guru: in Hinduism and Tibetan Buddhism, a personal, spiritual teacher; a trusted counselor and adviser; a mentor

Hieroglyphics: a system of writing in which pictorial symbols are used to represent meaning, sounds, or a combination of the two

Higgs Boson: the particle that gives mass to matter—also known as the God particle

Hubris: excessive pride; overbearing presumption; arrogance; dangerous overconfidence often in combination with arrogance

Human Consciousness: the state of being conscious; having an awareness of one's own existence, environment, sensations, and thoughts

Humanistic Materialism: a philosophy that is concerned with human beings, their achievement, and their interests, rather than with abstract beings and theology; based on only physical substance that can be observed, studied, and quantified rather than on abstractions that have not been scientifically established; a preoccupation with matter rather than anything intellectual or spiritual

Idealism, Idealistic (philosophy): in idealistic philosophy, the doctrine that ideas are the only permanent reality; mind is the essence of reality

Ideation, Ideational: of the nature of a notion or concept; pertaining to the formation of ideas or thoughts not immediately present to the senses

Idiot: formerly used to designate severe mental retardation, IQ below 20; now called profound intellectual disability

Ignominious: incurring public disgrace, shameful; characterized by or deserving shame or disgrace; degrading, debasing

Illusion: a misleading image; an erroneous perception of reality; an erroneous concept or belief

Imminent: about to occur; impending; near at hand

Incognito: with one's identity disguised or concealed; hiding one's true identity

Incorporate: to combine with something already in existence; to cause to merge or combine into a united whole

Indwelling: residing within; implanted; inner presence as of spirit or power

Infiltrate: penetrate, usually with hostile intent

Infinitude: having no boundaries, limits or end; impossible to measure or calculate

Infrared Light: electromagnetic radiation with wave longer than those of visible light; wavelengths from 1 millimeter to 700 nanometers; part of the magnetic spectrum; not visible to human eyes, but can be detected as heat (used by the remote controls on your TV and other gadgets);

Infrastructure: underlying base or foundation, especially for an organization or system

Inherent: existing as an essential constituent of something; permanently existing in something; inseparably attached or connected; innate

Integrate: to join with something else; to make part of a larger unit; to make whole by bringing parts together

Intention: determination to act in a certain way; an aim that guides action; an objective, purpose, or goal

Interplay: reciprocal action and reaction; interaction; mutual action or influence

Intractable: difficult to deal with or change to an acceptable condition; unyielding; difficult to alleviate, cure, or solve

Intrinsic: belonging to the essential nature of a thing; occurring as a natural part of something; inherent

Introspection: looking inward; mental self-examination; contemplation of one's own thoughts, feelings, and sensations

Juggernaut: overwhelming or unstoppable force; a literal or metaphorical force regarded as merciless, destructive, and unstoppable

Latent: being in a condition of rest or inactivity; present or potential, but not evident or active; present, but not symptomatic

Liberation: being freed from limiting concepts of bondage, restraint, or prevailing societal structures

Light Waves: a type of electromagnetic wave, some of which are visible and some invisible; comprised of energy from oscillating (moving to and fro like a swing) magnetic and electrical fields

Literal: Limited to the simplest or most obvious meaning of something; avoiding exaggeration, metaphor, or embellishment; factual

Locus: position, point, or place; a location where everything is centered; the center of activity or concentration

Macrocosm: the entire world, the universe; a system reflecting on a large scale one of its component systems or parts

Manifest: clearly apparent to sight or understanding; readily perceived by the senses; evident

Manifold: marked by diversity or variety; multifaceted

Mass (physics): a quantitative measure of inertia (a fundamental property of all matter)—inertia is the quality of matter that lets it stay still if it is still, or keeps it moving if it is moving

Materialism, Materialistic, Realism (philosophy): in materialistic philosophy, the doctrine that material objects are independent of the human mind and can exist on their own; everything in the universe is made from physical material including the mind or brain, and spiritual attributes do not exist in the universe

Maxwell's Equation: a set of coupled partial differential equations that, together with the Lorentz Force Law, form the foundation of classical electromagnetism, classical optics, and electric circuits; a dynamic theory of the electromagnetic field; has wide-ranging applications

Mediate (physics): to act as a go-between, between two quarks; a force is acted on each quark due to the presence of the other

Metaphor: figure of speech in which a word or phrase that ordinarily designates one thing is used to designate another; a symbol that implies comparison by transfer of terms as in "a sea of trouble" or "drowning in money"

Metaphysics: the study of things beyond the description of physical systems such as the contemplation and awareness of existence; study of things like being, existence, purpose, causality, etc.; includes ontology and cosmology among many other abstract concepts; accepts as valid but transcends all specific religions

Methodology: a body of methods, rules, and postulates employed by a particular discipline, a particular field of study

Microcosm: a small representative system having analogies to a larger system in its constitution, configuration, or development; a small subset of the whole generally considered to be representative of the whole

Microtubules: microscopic, hollow tubes made of alpha and beta tubulin that are part of the cell's cytoskeleton and are extended throughout the cell; thought by some to be related to consciousness

Microwaves: comparatively short electromagnetic wave radiations

Mitigate: to relieve or alleviate some situation or thing to make it less severe

Miracles: supernatural events that are not explainable by nature or science: exceed the productive power of nature as we know it

Monotheistic: pertaining to the doctrine or belief that there is only one God

Muons: unstable elementary particles, having similar properties to the electron, but with a mass 207 times greater; exist in negative and positive forms

Mythical: legendary narrative that explains a practice or a natural phenomenon (embodying cultural ideals and deep commonly held emotions)

Negate/negation: make ineffective or invalid; nullify; denial, contradiction, or negative statement

Neurobiologist: scientist who studies living organisms—the anatomy, physiology, and pathology of the nervous system, including the cells of the nervous system

Neuron: fundamental unit of the nervous system specialized to transmit information to different parts of the body; structural and functional unit of the nervous system of most vertebrates and invertebrates

Neurosis: a psychological state characterized by excessive anxiety or insecurity compensated for by the use of defense mechanisms

Neutrino: an elementary particle classified as a lepton; has an extremely small mass that may even be zero and no electric charge; interacts with its surrounding only via the weak force or gravity

Neutron: an uncharged elementary particle that has a mass nearly equal to that of the proton and is present in all known atomic nuclei except the hydrogen nucleus

Newtonian Physics: description of mechanical events involving forces that act on matter using the laws of motion and gravitation formulated in the late 17th century by Sir Isaac Newton

Nihilism: the doctrine that nothing actually exists or that existence or values are meaningless; relentless negativity or cynicism suggesting an absence of values or beliefs; political actions that advocate or commit violence without constructive goals

Nirvana: a place of perfect peace and happiness; the result of the extinction of individual passion, hatred, and division; freedom from the endless cycle of personal reincarnations with their consequent suffering (a key tenet of Buddhism)

Nodal: pertaining to or of the nature of a node (a node is a centering point of component parts where two things come together)

Nonlocality: influence between distant space-like separated systems; particles "know" the states of other particles (even at great distance) and correlate their behavior with each other instantaneously; called "spooky actions at a distance" by Albert Einstein (makes more sense if you have a nonmaterialist view of the world)

Nothingness: philosophical term for general state of nonexistence, absence of anything, physical or metaphysical

Nucleus: central or essential part around which other parts are gathered or are grouped; a core; a double membrane eukaryotic cell organelle that contains the genetic material

Nullify: invalidate; to deprive of efficacy; to counteract the force or effectiveness of something; to make void

Obeisance: an attitude of deference or homage; expressing obedience and respect; the power or right to demand obedience

Objective: existing independent of the mind; actual, real; based on observable phenomena; material, measurable, knowable, quantifiable

Obliterate: remove all signs of something

Omnipresent: present everywhere simultaneously; God is described as being omnipresent

Ontological: relating to the nature or essence of being; the branch of metaphysics that studies the nature of being as such

Panpsychism (psychology): the view that mind or a mind-like aspect is a fundamental and ubiquitous feature of reality

Paradox/Paradoxical: a statement that seems to contradict itself, but may nonetheless be true; self-contradictory statement or logically untenable statement, although based on a valid deduction from acceptable premises; a person or thing that exhibits inexplicable or contradicting aspects

Parity: equality; similarity or close correspondence or equivalence as regards state, position, condition quality, degree, etc.

Particles (physics): in quantum physics, particles are the smallest scales of energy at the atomic and subatomic levels, are located to specific spots, and move in accordance with Newtonian laws of motion; constituting matter and radiation

Pathology: a departure or deviation from a normal condition; an anatomic or a functional manifestation of disease

Penetrate: to pass into or through something by overcoming resistance

Perception: thought, belief, or opinion based on the appearance of something by means of the senses of the mind; a state of awareness of something

Per se: of, in, or by itself intrinsically

Perspective: a mental view or outlook; a way of regarding a situation and judging the relative importance of it; the ability to see the proper or accurate point of view in a situation

Phantom (physics): hypothetical form of dark energy satisfying the equation of a state with <; it possesses negative kinetic energy and predicts an expansion of the universe in excess of that predicted by a cosmological constant

Phenomena: things that exist and can be seen, felt, tasted, etc.; things that are observable, especially interesting or unusual things

Phenomenology: philosophy or method of inquiry based on the premise that reality consists of objects and events as they are perceived and understood in human consciousness and not of anything independent of human consciousness; structures of consciousness experienced from the first-person point of view

Philosophy: the study of general and fundamental questions such as those about existence, reason, knowledge, value, mind, and language

Photon: a type of elementary particle; the quantum of the electromagnetic field including electromagnetic radiation such as light and radio waves, and the force carrier for the electromagnetic force; massless—always moving at the speed of light in a vacuum

Photosynthesis: the process whereby plants, algae, and some types of bacteria capture energy from the sunlight to produce oxygen and chemical energy stored in glucose (herbivores then obtain this energy by eating plants, and carnivores obtain it from eating herbivores)

Physical Cosmos: the physical situation that is the context in the large for human existence; the world or universe as a complex and ordered system

Pions (physics): any of three least massive mesons, having a positive, neutral, or negative charge; a meson involved in holding a nucleus together; produced as the result of a high energy particle collision

Pivotal: vitally important; having a major function or effect

Polarize: to cause something to divide; to split into two sides that are so different it seems as though they are opposites like the North and South Poles on the earth

Polymath: a person of varied encyclopedic learning; a person with broad and comprehensive knowledge

Polytheistic: believing in or worshipping multiple gods

Precepts: rules or principles prescribing a particular course of action or conduct; directions issued by an authority

Preeminent: well-known and well-respected; superior to or notable above all others; outstanding, paramount in dignity or importance; supreme

Premise: a proposition upon which an argument is based; either the major or minor proposition of a syllogism from which a conclusion is drawn

Preposterous: contrary to nature, reason, or common sense; absurd, foolish

Probability: the quality of being probable; the likelihood that a given event will occur; numerical description of how likely an event is to occur

Proclamation: something made publicly known by a person of authority; an announcement or declaration

Profound: difficult to fathom or understand; having intellectual depth and insight

Progenitor: direct ancestor; originator of a line of descent; a founder

Proton: an elementary particle identical with the nucleus of the hydrogen atom, that along with the neutron is a constituent of all other atomic nuclei carrying a positive charge numerally equal to the charge of an electron

Psyche: the totality of the human mind, conscious and unconscious

Psychoactive: affecting the mind, mood, or mental processes; also used to describe drugs that cause these effects

Psychosocial: involving aspects of both social and psychological behavior

Psychology: the science of mind and behavior; includes conscious and unconscious phenomena as well as feeling and thought; includes study of the emergent properties of brains, linking the discipline to neuroscience

Psychologist: person who studies mind and behavior in the treatment of mental, emotional, and behavioral disorders

Psychoanalysis: a systematic structure of theories concerning the relation of conscious and unconscious psychological processes; a method of analyzing psychic phenomena and treating emotional disorders

Psychopathic: having the behavior and personality traits of a psychopath; suffering from a mental disorder or psychosis

Psychophysical: relating to the scientific study of the relationship between physical stimuli and the perceptions they produce and the relationship between physical stimuli and sensory response

Psychosis: an acute or chronic condition that affects the mind where there is a loss of contact with reality; a change in the field of consciousness

Pundits: critics, sources of opinion; learned persons

Quantum Dynamics: a branch of quantum mechanics that deals with interactions between moving particles at quantum scale

Quantum Mechanics: foundation of all quantum physics; provides a description of physical properties at the scale of atoms and subatomic particles

Quantum Physics: the branch of physics that uses quantum theory to describe the properties of a physical system, such as the behavior and structure of atoms and molecules; used especially with the microcosm (the behavior of matter and energy at the atomic level); the study of the minimum amount of physical entity involved in an interaction

Quantum Realm: also called the quantum scale, where mechanical effects become important when studied in an isolated system

Quantum Structure: quantum mechanics used for fabricating high frequency devices with enhanced performance

Quantum Theory: a theory describing energy in discrete levels or packets called quanta, and the consequent probabilistic behavior of atoms and subatomic particles

Quarks: up and down quarks make up the protons and neutrons seen in the nucleus of ordinary matter (up and down quarks are lightest and most stable; heavier quarks are produced by high energy collisions and rapidly decay into up and down quarks)

Quietude: peacefulness, tranquility, stillness, serenity, calmness

Radical: reaching toward the center—the ultimate sources; carried to the farthest limits, extreme, sweeping

Radioactive decay: a process whereby an unstable atomic nucleus loses energy by radiation; heat is released as a result of radioactive decay; any material containing an unstable nucleus is considered radioactive (also called nuclear decay, radioactivity, radioactive disintegration, or nuclear disintegration)

Radium: intensely radioactive element found in very small amounts in uranium ores; a chemical element of very remarkable character; emits alpha particles and gamma rays to form radon, which is used in the treatment of cancer and in radiographic devices

Ransom: a consideration paid or demanded for the release of someone or something from captivity. In Christianity, redemption from sin and its consequences

Reciprocity: a mutual interchange of something; mutual dependence, action, or influence

Reductionism (philosophy): an approach to the nature of complex things by reducing them to the interactions of their parts or to simpler, more fundamental things

Reductionism (physics): an attempt to reduce explanations to smaller constituents and to explain phenomena in terms of the relations of the constituents

Reincarnation: rebirth of the soul in another human or nonhuman body; a reappearance in a new form; the act of being incarnated again and again (a tenet of Buddhism and Hinduism)

Reintegration: a renewing of making whole again; restoration of unity

Relativity, Theory of: two interrelated theories developed by Albert Einstein, Special Relativity and General Relativity. General Relativity explains the law of gravitation and its relation to other forces of nature while Special Relativity applies to all physical phenomena in the absence of gravity

Renaissance: transitional movement in Europe between medieval and modern times, approximately 1350–1620 AD; associated with great social change

***Res cogitantes* (thinking entities):** thinking entities, mind; mind is viewed as a substance distinct from the physical world

Res extensae (**extended entities**): extended things; referring to material substances, the physical realm of matter; everything physical in the material world

Residency: settled in a place intended to be permanent; official place of residence; dwelling in a place for a long time

Resilience (psychology): the ability to rebound from adversity by virtue of inner mental strength; to be able to face tragedy, trauma, and adversity with courage and fortitude

Resolution: the correction of a problem or problems; act of resolving or solving a problem; a course of action determined or decided upon

Residue: the remainder of something after the removal of a part or parts; from Old French *residu,* meaning staying behind, residing

Revelations: things newly revealed; sudden insights; dramatic disclosures of things not previously known or realized

Revelatory: serving to reveal something; showing or disclosing an emotion, belief, or quality, or the like; prophetic

Rudimentary: of or relating to basic facts or principles; elementary: set apart for sacred use; make holy; purify; free from moral guilt or blemish

Sentience: the capacity to experience feelings and sensations

Singular: the form of a word used when talking about one thing

Singularity (physics): a point where some property is infinite; a time/space singularity is where the quantities that are used to measure the gravitational field become useless; a point in time/space where the laws of physics as we know them break down; a point at which all physical laws cease to have any independent meaning

Socialist: a person who espouses any of various economic and political theories advocating collective or governmental ownership and administration of the means of the production and distribution of goods

Socialist Equalizing Theories: a number of theories that attempt to "level the playing field"; attempt to achieve equality, equity, or equal outcomes (antithetical to freedom and free will)

Socioeconomic: of or relating to the interaction of social and economic factors

Sociology: the study of human social relationships and institutions; the systematic study of the development, structure, interaction, and collective behavior of organized groups of humans

Sociopathic: having no concern about the adverse consequences on other people as a result of one's actions; a personality disorder

Solidarity (physics): binding together into a unity, cohesive oneness

Sovereignty: supremacy of authority; having supreme power or authority over all others

Status: high standing, prestige; position relative to the position of others

Stimulus-Response: when any part of an organism is stimulated, a reaction or response will occur; a belief by Behaviorists that the use of rewards and punishments leads to changes in behavior

Stipulate: state exactly how something must be done; specify explicitly the essential conditions in terms of agreement

Strong Force (one of the four forces of physics): the short-range attractive force that holds together the nucleus of the atom; binds quarks together to make subatomic particles such as protons and neutrons; a process of particle creation in high energy collisions; the strongest known fundamental physical force, but acts only over distances comparable to those between nucleons in an atomic nucleus

Structure: the way in which parts are put together to make a whole; the interrelation or arrangement of parts in a complex entity; something made up of a number of parts that are put together

Subjective: existing in the mind; belonging to the thinking subject rather than to the object of the thought; qualitative, open to interpretation

Succinctly: expressed with concise and precise brevity; to the point; clearly, without unnecessary words

Sumerian: one of the first known cultures of the world along with ancient Egypt, the Minoans, and others

Supersede: replace or supplant in power, authority, effectiveness, etc. by another person or thing

Supernova: a large explosion that takes place at the end of a star's life

Symmetry (physics): a property that remains the same even after some kind of transformation has been performed; the properties of particles such as atoms and molecules remain unchanged after being subjected to a variety of symmetry transformations or "operations" (quantum mechanics and the theory of relativity have notions of symmetry)

Synthesis: the combining of separate elements or substances to form a coherent whole; combining a number of different parts or ideas to come up with a new idea or theory

Systemic: of or affecting something in its entirety; something that affects the whole, not just parts

Terahertz Rays: radiation between microwaves and infrared frequencies on the electromagnetic spectrum with frequencies from 03 to 10 Terahertz

The Great Divide: the mind-body split; the division of that which is subjective (thinking) from that which is objective (matter)

Theoretical: a proposal to see a phenomenon in a certain way; relating to or consisting in theory rather than practice; ideas that cannot be simply reduced to describing a set of observations

Thesis: a proposition maintained by argument; a hypothetical proposition, especially one put forward without proof

Transactional Analysis: a system of psychotherapy that analyzes personal relationships and interactions in terms of conflicting or complementary ego states that correspond to roles of parent, child, adult

Transcendent: reaching beyond the limits of human knowledge and intellect; above and independent of the material universe

Transmitted: sent from one person, place, or thing to another person, place, or thing

Transmitters: things that transmit information by working together; devices that generate and amplify a carrier wave, modulate it with a meaningful signal and radiate the resulting signal

Transpose: to change in form or nature, transform; to change the relative position or order of something

Tubules: hollow cylindrical structures in the cytoplasm of most cells; involved in intracellular shape and transport

Ultraviolet Light: an electromagnetic wave that cannot be perceived by human eyes, but exists everywhere

Uncertainty Principle: also known as the Heisenberg uncertainty principle; is based on the wave/particle duality of matter (can be ignored in the macro world but holds significant value in the quantum world)

Unified Duality: two parts of a single entity functioning together as one

Utopian: a society in which the inhabitants of a place live and work together in a place of perfect harmony and happiness; a visionary reform that tends to be impossibly idealistic and unattainable

Venue: place or opportunity for communicating ideas and information; location in which something takes place

Verify: to prove the truth or accuracy of something; to demonstrate the truth or accuracy of something, as by the presentation of evidence

Visible Light (physics): the segment of the electromagnetic spectrum the human eye can see; wavelengths from 380 to 700 nanometers

Wave (physics): transports energy, not matter; particles do not travel with waves; a disturbance or variation that travels through a medium from one location to another; examples are ocean waves, light waves, earthquake waves, stringed instrument waves

Wave/Particle duality: light interacts with electrons as a particle; it can behave as a particle and as a wave as evidenced by the photoelectric effect that can be measured

Weak Force (one of the four forces of physics): a force through which particles interact with each other; plays a key role in radioactive decay; one of the four fundamental forces

X-rays: penetrating forms of high-energy electromagnetic radiation; can pass though objects, including the human body

Bibliography

Don read many of these books in their entirety and used others as reference material.

Aczal, Amir D., *Why Science Does Not Disprove God*
William Morrow, 2014

Appleyard, Bryan, *Understanding the Present: Science and the Soul of Modern Man*
Doubleday, 1992

Barbour, Ian G., *Religion and Science*
Harper, San Francisco, 1997

Behe, Michael, *The Edge of Evolution*
Free Press, 2007

Berlinski, David, *The Devil's Delusion: Atheism and Its Scientific Pretensions*
Perseus Books Group, N.Y. 2009

Block, Ned, Flanagan, Owen, & Guzeldere, Guven, Editors, *The Nature of Consciousness*
Massachusetts Institute of Technology, 1997

Carroll, Sean, *The Particle at the End of the Universe*
Plume, 2012

Chalmers, David J., *The Conscious Mind*
Oxford University Press, 1966

Chalmers, David J., *The Character of Consciousness*
Oxford University Press, 2010

Davies, Paul, *The Mind of God*
Simon and Schuster, 1992

Davies, Paul, *God and the New Physics*
Simon and Schuster, 1983

Davies, Paul, *The New Physics*
Simon and Schuster, 1996

Davies, Paul, *The Cosmic Blueprint*
Templeton Foundation Press, 1998

Dawkins, Richard, *The God Delusion*
Penguin Books, 2020

Dawkins, Richard, *The Greatest Show on Earth*
Simon and Schuster, 2009

Demski, Wm. A., Editor, *Uncommon Dissent*
ISI Books, 2004

Demski, Wm., *The Design Revolution*
American Catholic Philosophical Quarterly, 2004

Edwards, Paul, Editor in Chief, *The Encyclopedia of Philosophy, V. 1–8*
Macmillan Publishing Co. Inc. and The Free Press, 1967

Greene, Brian, *The Elegant Universe*
W.W. Norton, 2003

Greene, Brian, *The Fabric of the Cosmos*
Vintage, 2005

Hawking, Stephen, *A Brief History of Time,* **and** *The Universe in a Nutshell*
Bantam Dell Books, 1996

Harris, Sam, *The End of Faith*
W.W. Norton & Company, 2004

Horgan, John, *The End of Science*
Addison-Wesley Publishing Company, 1996

Isaacson, Walter, *Einstein, His Life and Universe*
Simon and Schuster, 2001

Kaku, Michio, *Physics of the Impossible*
Anchor Books, 2008

Kaku, Michio, *The Future of the Mind*
Anchor Books, 2014

Kierkegaard, Søren, *The Concept of Anxiety,* **Translated by Thomte, Reidar & Anderson, Albert B.**
Princeton University Press, 1980

Kierkegaard, Søren, *The Sickness unto Death*, Translated by Hong, Howard V. & Edna H.
Princeton University Press, 1980

Kierkegaard, Søren, *The Concept of Anxiety*, Translated by Lowrie, Walter
Princeton University Press, 1957

Lanza, Robert, *Beyond Biocentrism*
Ben Bella Books, 2016

Kumar, Manjit, *Quantum*
Wm. Norton, 2010

Lanza, Robert, *The Grand Biocentric Design*
BenBella Books, 2020

Lederman, Leon & Hill, Christopher, *Beyond the God Particle*
Prometheus Books, 2013

Lederman, Leon & Hill Christopher, *Quantum Physics for Poets*
Prometheus Books, 2011

Lederman, Leon & Hill, Christopher, *Symmetry and the Beautiful Universe*
Prometheus Books, 2004

Lennox, John C., *God's Undertaker*
Gutenberg Press, 2009

Meyer, Stephen, *The Signature in the Cell*
Harper Collins, 2013

Meyer, Stephen, *Darwin's Doubt*
Harper Collins, 2013

Nicholi, Armand M. Jr., *The Question of God: The C.S. Lewis & Sigmund Freud Debate*
Gutenberg Press, 2002

Overman, Dean, *A Case Against Accident and Self-Organization*
Rowman and Littlefield, 1997

Pascal, Blaise, *Pascal's Pensées*
E.P. Dutton & Company, 1958 Edition

Penrose, Sir Roger, Hameroff, Stuart, & Kak, Subhash, *Consciousness and the Universe*
Cosmology Science Publishers, 2009, 2010, 2011

Polkinghorne, John, *Exploring Reality*
Yale University Press, 2005

Polkinghorne. John, *Quantum Physics and Theology*
Yale University Press, 2007

Polkinghorne, John, *Quarks, Chaos and Christianity*
Crossroad Publishing, 2005

Polkinghorne, John, *Questions of Truth*
John Knox Press, 2009

Popper, Karl R. & Eccles, John C., *The Self and Its Brain*
Routledge, London & N.Y. 1977

Schroeder, Gerald, *The Hidden Face of God*
Touchstone, 2001

Schwartz. Jeffrey M, *The Mind and Its Brain*
Harper Collins, 2002

Searle, John R, *The Mystery of Consciousness*
Granta Books, London, 1998

Smith, Huston, *The World's Religions*
Harper, San Francisco, 1991

Smith, Huston, *Why Religion Matters*
Harper, San Francisco, 2001

Smith, Wolfgang, The Wisdom of Ancient Cosmology
Foundation for Traditional Studies, 2003

Smith, Wolfgang, *Cosmos and Transcendence*
Sophia Perennis, 2008

Smith, Wolfgang, *The Quantum Enigma*
Sophia Perennis, 2008

Smith, Wolfgang, *Science and Myth*
Sophia Perennis, 2010

Stapp, Henry P, *The Mindful Universe, Second Edition*
Springer, 2011

Tarnas, Richard, *The Passion of the Western Mind*
Ballantine Books, N.Y., 1993

Tillich, Paul, *The Courage to Be*
Yale University Press, 1952

Tillich, Paul, *Systematic Theology*
Chicago University Press, 1965

About the Illustrations

Chapter One—*The Great Divide*

Caption: *The Great Divide*

The angel represents spirituality; the measuring device represents the physical existential world. This illustration was adapted by Lauren Winkle from an engraving entitled "Melancholia'" by the German artist Albrecht Durer (1471-1494).

Chapter Two—*Consciousness*

Caption: *Consciousness*

This mezzotint by Jon Ogard portrays the transcendental nature of human consciousness. It depicts a sleeping human whose consciousness is not confined to his body.

Chapter Three—*The Existential Dilemma*

Caption: *Quiescence*

The human face in the mountain symbolizes a human being who seems calm on the outside, but who is troubled by inherent anxiety that may suddenly become debilitating and ruinous, just as the face of a mountain may conceal a seething cauldron inside. Lithograph by Jon Ogard.

Caption: *The Scream* **(Anxiety)**

This iconic image by Norwegian artist Edvard Munch (1863-1944) was created in 1893 and is believed to portray inherent anxiety. According to Munch's own account, he was walking along a street in Oslo above the fjord when the sky turned red and he suddenly sensed an infinite scream running through all of nature. This adaptation of the painting was created by Lauren Winkle.

Chapter Four—The Search for a Solution in Religion

Caption: *Spiritual Quests*

The search for spiritual, transcendent meaning is depicted by symbols of four great religious traditions. The lotus blossom of Hinduism is a symbol of purity, rebirth, and enlightenment. The Dharma Wheel of Buddhism represents the eightfold path to a transformative spiritual life. The Star of David, for Judaism, is a symbol of the protective shield of God over King David. The origins of the crescent moon and star are obscure, but the combination has become widely portrayed as a symbol of Islam—a crescent moon marks the proper days, such as Ramadan, for a period of prayer and fasting. Lauren Winkle created the image.

Chapter Five—The Search for a Solution in Philosophy, Psychology, and Sociology

Caption: *Secular Quests*

The image of a thinking man, executed in pen and ink by Lowell Hinrichs, Kathleen Ogard's brother, depicts earnest secular searches for solutions to the Existential Dilemma in the fields of philosophy, psychology, sociology, and social work.

Caption: *The Tree in the Quad*
The image—a pencil drawing by Joel Ogard—along with the limerick, may lead us to ponder the nature of reality and to ask ourselves the question: "In the final analysis, is the metaphysical realm actually more real than the physical?"

Caption: *Humpty Dumpty*
This drawing by Lauren Winkle illustrates one of her grandfather's favorite nursery rhymes, which he quoted frequently. Don believed that some professionals in the fields of psychology, social work, and sociology believed they could resolve the dilemma for human beings through an interface between professionals and personal and societal problems. Futile, in Don's opinion!

Chapter Six

Caption: *So . . . How Shall We Live?*
The wondering, contemplating eyes in this lithograph by Jon Ogard depict the efforts of human beings to somehow work out how to live out their lives in this puzzling, existential world.

Caption: *Living with the Existential Dilemma*
This graph was drawn by Don in paper and pencil and executed for this book by Lauren Winkle. The arrows in the quadrant can move in either direction because life is fluid and subject to conscious and unconscious choices by each individual.

Chapter Seven—the Quantum Enigma

Caption: *The Thinker*

French sculptor Auguste Rodin (1840-1917) is believed to be the founder of modern sculpture. This larger-than-life depiction of a man deep in thought and concentration was first modeled in clay and then cast in bronze. There are many castings of this famous statue all over the Western world.

Chapter Eight—The Jesus Enigma

Caption: *Given for You* (Luke 22:19)

The chalice was drawn in pencil by Joel Ogard. The indistinct face of Jesus was suggested by the Shroud of Turin, which some believe to be the burial cloth of Jesus. The image is a negative of a crucified man on a shroud discovered in 1578 in Turin, Italy. Joel used it to suggest the presence of the risen Christ in our lives.

The Gordian Knot

Caption: *The Gordian Knot*

The Gordian Knot represents a seemingly intractable problem. According to legend, Alexander the Great came to a city whose gate was barred by an ox cart tied to the city gate with a knot that no one was able to untie. Alexander simply took out his sword and cut the knot off, thus enabling his entry into the city. The drawing is by Lauren Winkle.

Chapter Nine—The Words of Jesus

Caption: *"I am the Way, the Truth, and the Life."* (John 14:6)

The calligraphic design was created by Lauren Winkle.

Chapter Ten—The Works of Jesus

Caption: *"Ask and it will be given to you."* (Matthew 7:7)

This famous depiction of hands in prayer is from an engraving by Albrecht Durer, who also created the image of the angel in Chapter One.

Chapter Eleven—The Triumph of Faith

Caption: *"Behold, I stand at the door and knock."* (Revelation 3:20)

Joel Ogard produced this drawing in pencil to illustrate the truth that Jesus still knocks at the doors of human hearts today and always.

The Jesus Enigma 2 (Smaller image of the chalice appearing at the beginning of Chapter Eight)

Caption: *"This do in remembrance of me."*

The image reminds us of Jesus' sacrifice for us and also reminds us that Jesus is present with us always, as he promised. Drawing by Joel Ogard.

About the Author

Donald W. Ogard (1920-2021)

A lifelong student of human behavior, Don Ogard received a Bachelor's degree from Pacific Lutheran University and a Master of Social Work degree from the University of Washington.

Don served as a counselor and therapist for over 40 years. His focus was on identifying sources of anxiety and helping people to understand and manage it. He also taught Social Work and Sociology at Concordia University as an adjunct professor.

In Don's later years, he studied and wrote on such wide-ranging topics as psychology, theology, and quantum physics, to name a few. The Existential Dilemma, published posthumously, is a culmination of Don's studies, grappling with the tough topics of the origin of human consciousness and existential anxiety.

Don and his wife of 65 years, Kathleen, made their home in Portland, Oregon, where Don maintained his counseling practice and enjoyed hiking, woodworking, and watching his children and grandchildren's sports games and events. The Ogards have four children and 10 grandchildren.

Printed in the USA
CPSIA information can be obtained
at www.ICGtesting.com
LVHW071441121123
763715LV00059B/1175